# 2GRIEVE 2GETHER

God bless &
keep you~

*[signature]*

# 2GRIEVE 2GETHER

## A JOURNAL FROM THE HEART
## HELPING SURVIVORS & SUPPORTERS
## NAVIGATE THE HEALING PROCESS

*by*

DENISE HALL BROWN

2Grieve 2Gether: A Journal from the Heart Helping Survivors and
Supporters Navigate the Healing Process

Copyright © 2011 by Denise Hall Brown

ISBN 978-0-9833170-0-5

Printed in the USA by 2 Lift 1 Up Publishing

# CONTENTS

# ACKNOWLEDGMENTS

THIS book was written with love, appreciation and reverence for:

**Carolyn P. Hall Jones** – June 26, 1945 to June 2, 1995: You were not only my mother, but also my friend. You were the first person I turned to in good times and bad, because I knew you'd tell me what I needed to hear while loving me through it all. Your encouragement (and discipline) is evident in everything I accomplish. Thanks for leaving me with your wisdom, spirit, and freckles, along with a daughter (my sister) who keeps your memory and love alive!

**Isaiah Charles Brown** – April 7, 2005 to September 8, 2005: You, my little angel, came to show me what love was all about, and how much God cares for all of us. "Those who wait on the Lord shall renew their strength; They shall mount up with wings like eagles; They shall run and not be weary; They shall walk and not faint." –Isaiah 40:31 (New King James Version). Thank you for providing me with hope. I look forward to holding you in my arms again in the next life!

**Flora M. Jones Snowden** – September 21, 1943 to January 6, 2007: You loved me like a daughter and I would give anything to go shopping and have dinner with you just one more time. Boy did we laugh! Thank you for putting up with me and giving me so much love, even when it was difficult for me to receive that love. While I miss you greatly, I take solace in knowing that you and your beloved sisters and parents are together again!

**Ralph Coleman Brown Jr.** – April 4, 1960 to June 12, 2009: I thank God for putting two imperfect people together and creating a perfect love that produced four wonderful sons and a legacy that will last forever. Thank you for being a wonderful role model for our children, taking care of me, and being strong enough for both of us. As your last card to me said, "True love is eternal." I now know that it is, and, Ralph, I will love and honor you for the rest of my life!

# DEDICATION

THIS book is humbly and lovingly dedicated to:

**Tre, William, and Malcolm Brown** – Sons, you are a living legacy to all who have come and gone before you, as well as those who still have the privilege to be part of your lives. When I look at you as young men, I am amazed at how much loss you've experienced at such early ages and how well you have adapted. I am so honored to be your mother! As you go forward and live productive lives, know that there will be peaks and valleys throughout life, but that you can and will make it through. Know that the trials and pain you face are not a reflection of God's love for you. Instead, know that His love is reflected as He helps you make it through every loss, trial, and setback you encounter. Most of all, know that you have some very special angels watching over you, and that you have a really proud mama who will encourage and love you forever!

**All Survivors Who Are Hurting or Supporters Who Are Reaching Out to Help Others** – If you purchased this book, you are either a Survivor or Supporter, and you've taken a step toward healing and/or helping. Thank you for allowing me to share my ongoing journey with you. That connection truly aids me in my own healing process. My prayer for you is that you will heal or help as you accept the challenge "to grieve together"!

# PREFACE

UNFORTUNATELY, I know grief well. It has been an unwelcome companion over the last fifteen years. While I'd faced the deaths of my grandparents, an uncle, and my husband's parents, nothing prepared me for June of 1995—the month when I was to turn thirty, and my mom would have reached the milestone of fifty beautiful years. On the second day of that month, a drunk driver crossed the center line and changed all of our lives. In an instant, the woman who gave me life and light was gone. My sister, who was also in the car, survived the accident, but neither of us was ever the same. I can candidly say I lost my mind following my mom's death, and it took me three full years to get back to a "new normal." But I was never again the carefree young lady I'd been before the accident. Grief has a way of doing that. The experience also accelerated my spiritual development and taught me the benefit of therapy! I thought Mom's passing was the worst that could happen to me, until September 2005 when my five-month old son died as a result of a tragic accident. I can tell you that there's an incredible amount of pain associated with picking out a coffin for your child, no matter what age. This time, not only did I have to work through the pain, but I had three young children (then ages seven, ten, and thirteen) who I had to worry about, along with a husband who was in unbelievable mental and physical agony. We all received counseling and began to heal together. Just as I came out of the darkest period of that tragedy, January 2007 marked the loss of my mom's sister. My closest aunt was hit and killed instantly by someone who was drag racing. It was uncanny that the death of my aunt hit me almost as hard as that of my mom. I spent a lot of time obsessing over her death, yet it was hard to share that with others because she wasn't my mother. As such, there were a lot of thoughts going through my mind that I never shared with anyone. Most recently, in June 2009, my heart was broken again when my husband died unexpectedly from a lifelong medical condition. Nothing could have prepared me to say goodbye to my soul mate so soon. I still have days when I'm in total shock and absolutely cannot believe that he's gone from this earth. We had planned for so much more time together!

With so much heartache and pain, I believe I have two choices. First, I can wallow in it and ask "why me." Because I'm human, I admit there are days when I do that. But a larger portion of my days are spent embracing a second choice. I draw strength from my faith and find ways to bring some good out of a bad situation, which is why I've spent countless hours studying grief and meditating on what I could do to help myself and others. After my son Isaiah's death, I developed "grief cards" with a few notes on how to make it through grief and how to respond to those who are grieving. I did this because I had struggled so much in my grief and, on top of that, so many people didn't know how to respond to us. As a result, we were unintentionally hurt by some of their words, actions, or lack of both. The community's response to the cards and a related Web site was extremely positive. After my husband's death, I started reading more and saw the need for a book that acknowledged the power of relationships and resources in the healing process. It began with the concept of 2Grieve 2Gether, which acknowledges that healing is a process that shouldn't happen alone. At the same time that my head was thinking about a book, my heart was telling me to let out all of the emotions that were bottled up inside me. That led me to journaling. I started my diary in November 2009, after my sons attended a camp for grieving children where part of their activities included writing a letter to their deceased loved one. When they read their letters to me, I was reminded of the healing power of writing things down. And so, I did the same thing and found the same result: restoration!

With the encouragement of friends and an internal drive to help others, this book came together rather naturally. It includes both the resources I uncovered and my journal, along with the learning that came to light after I reflected on each entry. This book is not an all-encompassing picture of what grief looks like for everyone. Instead, it's merely a brief glimpse into my life as I tried to find meaning, peace, and healing. I pray that 2Grieve 2Gether underscores the importance of people helping themselves and others to deal with grief, a part of life that will affect each one of us.

# INTRODUCTION

**D**URING my times of mourning, I was touched by the kindness of strangers, the love of family, the bonds of friendship, and the eternal promises of God. Those relationships sustained me! At the same time, there were moments when I was clueless about what was "normal," how I should respond, and how I could ever make it through. In addition, there were people who didn't reach out during our periods of mourning, because they didn't know what to say or do. During this period, I got my hands on every resource available so I could understand myself and others. This book is dedicated to helping people who are hurting and includes information for people who are grieving (Survivors), as well as for those who want to reach out to help someone else (Supporters). This allows me to give back the wealth of love and friendship that was given to me during my seasons of grief. I am also reaching out, because in comforting others and increasing awareness, I am able to honor my loved ones. All that I have endured has not made me an expert in grief. I'd need a lot more study to reach that status. However, what I've gone through has made me empathetic and reflective. In looking back over my journey thus far, I've realized that my relationships with others (both people and God) and my desire to find resources to help (whether it's people, programs, or other things) is what has strengthened me. And so, my humble goal with this book is to be a conduit for you to identify and leverage the relationships and resources in your own life.

This book begins with thirty diary entries. The first two were written in December 2005. Three months after the passing of my five-month-old son, Isaiah, there was a night when I was really angry and decided to record my feelings. Specifically, I wrote about all the things that ticked me off. It was a very cleansing experience! A couple days later, I came back and wrote about the things that made me smile. Again, it was great for me. Four years later, as I dealt with the death of my husband, Ralph, I knew it was time for me to write again. This time, instead of a rant, I would write periodic letters to Ralph and other loved ones who had died. I decided to include whatever was on my mind. In addition, I included a couple of letters to God. It all just seemed to make sense for me. Those journal entries are included in this book. When I made the decision to share these entries with you, I looked at the many issues revealed in each entry and chose one general topic per entry to reflect on. I followed that up with questions for both Survivors and Supporters to consider, as well as some thoughts on actions that could be taken. I encourage the reader to ponder on one entry each day and have included space to record your thoughts and feelings, as well as what you will do.

As for me, in the future I will continue to write letters and deal with my ongoing struggles and triumphs as part of my healing process. I hope that the entries included herein provide you with a brief glimpse into my personal journey through grief, and in doing so, will lead you to embrace your own process or help someone else through theirs.

Following the first thirty chapters of journal entries are resources to assist both Survivors and Supporters, including suggestions on things you might do. I've also included helpful books, scriptures, Internet links, and many more resources on my Web site (www.2Grieve2Gether.org). Of course, the ideas are not all-inclusive, and I encourage you to begin creating your own resource lists. In fact, I'd love for you to share ideas with me. Feel free to send me an e-mail at denise@2Grieve2Gether.org.

Finally, whether you're grieving or trying to reach out to someone who is, remember that we experience everything in life as individuals. As such, no one set of suggestions will apply to every person or situation. I just hope this information can help you and/or someone you care about in some small way.

With love, respect and empathy,
Denise Hall Brown

# CHAPTER 1

# EXPRESSING EMOTIONS

*December 2005, written three months after Isaiah's death*

I am mad:

At all the insensitive people who thought enough of us to share their stupid Christmas letters/cards, but not enough to be sensitive to the fact that we've suffered a devastating loss and may not have the "holiday spirit".

At Ralph [my husband] for not being at home when he knows I hate to come home to an empty house.

At all my family members who didn't care enough about us to even call on Christmas, and most of whom haven't even spoken to us since the funeral.

At my so-called friends who didn't think enough of our relationship to call on Christmas.

At many of the same friends who I haven't even spoken to since the funeral.

At God for allowing our hearts to be broken like this and for surrounding me with friends who have babies born at the same time as Isaiah.

At myself for not remembering how it felt each time I held my baby.

At the fact that I'm the only person around who has suffered tragedies such as losing a child and having a mother killed by a drunk driver.

At myself for not visiting the grave enough and not making it a place where people can tell that our child was loved greatly.

At all those people who say they've been thinking about us, but never even call or write.

At the so-called Christians who've shown absolutely no Christian love.

At the fact that I even have to write something like this instead of spending this time spoiling my baby.

Because I have to go to a cemetery to visit one of my children.

That I got my tubes tied and can't have another child.

That my life is on public display and people are gossiping about us in the midst of our pain.

That my mom isn't here to help me through this.

That my children and those closest to me have suffered this loss too.

Because I'll never again have the joy I had during those five months.

**My Reflections**:

All these years later, I can still remember how angry and alone I felt that night. The feelings that overwhelmed me and that I expressed in writing were an outward sign of the pain I felt inside from losing a part of myself. I didn't really hate my friends, my family, my husband, or myself. I was just mad at the hand that life had dealt me, and I took it out on the easiest targets!

As I reflect on this entry, I now know that life is full of emotions, many of which are magnified when one is grieving. Why is it that we often feel guilty for expressing intense emotions? When a loved one dies, we may feel guilty for being angry about that fact. Then, we may feel guilty for having moments of happiness despite that special person being gone. It's almost a no-win proposition.

Why not change the paradigm? Why not realize that if we stuff our emotions down inside of us, at some point (and probably at the worst possible time) they will erupt? Why not let it out, be gentle with yourself, and move forward? Why not find a safe space to admit what you're feeling? I believe that in order to heal and adjust to the loss, it's important to allow ourselves to be human and to acknowledge the pain that comes with being separated from someone we loved dearly.

**Survivor Strategies**:

Think: What are you feeling? What are you holding in? What can you do to let your emotions out? Who will you trust to listen and empathize?

Do: Keep a log of your emotions. Each day (or several times during the day) write down your mood (happy, sad, confused, angry, depressed, grateful, etc.) and include notes on why you're feeling that way and/or what prompted the emotion. Review that log from time to time to assess and understand your journey.

**Supporter Strategies:**

Think: How can you encourage the Survivor to share his emotions? How can you listen without judgment and with lots of love and understanding? Because you may be grieving also, how will you find an outlet for your emotions?

Do: Keep your own journal of emotions and, at some point, share it with the Survivor as a way for the two of you to connect and to have additional dialogue and healing.

**Your Reflections:**

What's on your mind and in your heart after reading this entry and pondering the questions? In light of this, what will you do?

# Chapter 2

# Feeling Gratitude

*December 2005, written three months after the deth of my son, Isaiah, and a few days after "I am mad"*

I am glad:

That I got to spend five wonderful months with my baby, and during that time I did many of the things I should have done with the other three (stayed home longer, breast-fed for a longer period of time, took more pictures, took him wherever I went, and made him a central part of my life).

That my other three sons, Tre, William, and Malcolm, loved him so much and showed that love.

That my faith is growing stronger and my family is now committed to doing the things that will allow us to join Isaiah in heaven when our time comes.

That the relationship between my husband, Ralph, and me is growing stronger and not weaker.

That some of my friends have been such a blessing to me, because they lift me up and constantly support and love me.

That I have close family in my life to help me through this.

That the kids appear to be handling things and are able to talk about their brother with love.

That I have been able to take advantage of resources (such as therapy, books, support groups, and church), and that those things are helping me work through this process.

That it's okay to feel what I feel, that I don't have to be strong every minute of the day, and that my periods of sadness are okay.

Because I still have a future and so does my family.

Because I have forever been changed by a little angel who came to remind me of what unconditional love is and how it feels.

Because I know for sure that Isaiah is with God.

Because one day I will be with Isaiah again, and I'm no longer afraid of dying.

Because I know that God is with me every step of the way.

Because we're not doing many of the destructive things we could be doing (drinking, smoking, self-medicating, etc.) and are instead turning to each other and God.

**My Reflections**:

Reading this entry makes me smile, because it reminds me that in the midst of such a great tragedy I still found things for which I was grateful—something that isn't always easy for me to do. My earliest recollection of watching someone else grieve was when I was in high school. One of the nicest guys in school died from a freak accident. About a week later, I went to the local carnival and saw the student's brothers there. I remember coming home and asking my mom how they could attend a carnival when their brother had just died. She gently told me that life must go on, and I now know she was right.

Life continuing means that all parts of our lives continue, including joy, celebration, appreciation, and other feelings and activities that are positive. Just as those brothers had the courage to go on and smile at something as simple as a carnival, we too need to realize it is okay to be happy and appreciative. We may have moments when we cry or wallow in our loss, but may also see that it is natural to have moments when we smile, laugh, or partake in upbeat activities or emotions.

## Survivor Strategies:

Think: What are you grateful for? In what ways can you express that appreciation? How can you balance your wide variety of emotions?

Do: Try to think of at least one thing you're grateful for, and then begin a list that you add to periodically. Review it from time to time, and if you're willing to, share it with someone.

## Supporter Strategies:

Think: When the Survivor is ready, in what ways can you help her find something to be grateful for? Who can you enlist to help you?

Do: Make it a daily practice to think about what you're grateful for as a way to maintain your own balance and be in a stronger position to support the Survivor with her full range of emotions.

**Your Reflections:**

What's on your mind and in your heart after reading this entry and pondering the questions? In light of this, what will you do?

# CHAPTER 3

# EMBRACING
# SELF-CENTEREDNESS

*November 26, 2009, written five months after Ralph's death*

D EAR Ralph,

Happy Thanksgiving! What used to be good about this day is that it was one of the few days when we'd all be home together for at least two days in a row. I probably didn't appreciate that as much as I should have. I woke up this morning at 6:00 AM, a few minutes later than my body usually wakes me up. I can't say I'm feeling worse than usual today. It's just the same feeling of gloom I have each morning when I realize I'm the only one who occupies this bed.

You were in my dreams last night. Rarely do I remember the content of my dreams, but I know the feeling I have when I am certain that we were in each other's presence. I believe none of us really understands how this world operates. But I am certain that it wasn't just a dream. We were together. That being said, I still wish you were here physically so I could give you a hug, snuggle up against you, or jump on the bed and say something silly to wake you up. I know I'm still in shock. Despite your illness, I never ever thought you would leave me when you were just forty-nine years old. I thought we had forever! What a cruel thing for us to be separated when we were finally starting to understand each other and ourselves.

I will make sauerkraut for today's holiday dinner, as usual. I'll miss you lying around watching football. What will I complain about now? I think about all the times I nagged you to make sure you called your sisters (as if I couldn't do so on my own). So, this year I'll make sure to do it myself. I also think I'll invite them to dinner in a couple weeks, since it will be the six-month anniversary of your passing. I know you'd want us to be close and for the boys to stay in their lives.

Selfishly, I need to see your sisters, because I know they miss you as much as I do—especially Lynn, because she was your closest sister in age and she was really your best friend. I call her a lot just to talk about you and the things you used to do. I wonder if I talk about you too much to her, the kids, and everyone else.

It's almost like I worship you. What I really think is that I'm making up for the fact that I didn't appreciate you like I should have when you were alive. I definitely know I didn't tell you enough how great you were. Instead, I focused too much of my thoughts and energy on the negative. Now that I'm alone, all I can think of is the positive. I also think of how much I've lost.

How could I have been so foolish and so selfish? I was fortunate enough to have such a good husband, friend, and father for our children. Why didn't I know that at the time? Why do I always have to lose people to gain these insights? And how can I get God to stop the cycle of tragedy for this family and give us a break?

Boy do I wish you could speak to me from heaven. I wish God could speak to me. I can't hear His voice or yours. No wonder I feel such sadness every single day. This is true loneliness. I feel bad even expressing this, because I worry that God will take someone away from me again if I don't learn my lesson. I guess that sounds a little self-centered. I don't really care right this moment, because at least I'm finally being honest!

I'm so glad I started this habit of writing to you, because for some strange reason I feel like I'm being heard. Well, my love, on this Thanksgiving Day, I thank you for giving me our beautiful sons, for loving me despite my selfishness, for moving your life to my hometown so we could be together, and for all the beautiful memories you left with me. Please know that I love and miss you. Most of all, know that I will pour as much love as I can into our sons today.

**My Reflections:**

It is apparent in this entry that I was still in shock, five months after my husband's death. I imagine that those who interacted with me at that time would find it hard to believe that I was still struggling so much. That's because I was rather believable when I told people I was doing okay. I would quickly move conversations away from how I was doing and onto a much lighter topic. Yet, in those quiet moments alone at home, all I could think about was me and my situation. Generally, being self-centered is not a very attractive quality. However, there are times in life when we must acknowledge that if we don't help ourselves first, we may be unable to help others. That's actually less about being self-centered and more about being "self-caretaking."

Think about the instructions when you get on a plane. The stewardess tells you that if the worst happens, you must put your own air mask on first before you can assist others with theirs. The same is true in life and especially in grieving. Begin with an inward focus on your own needs and eventually you will be clear enough to focus on the external. That focus includes an honest assessment of where you are, how you're feeling, and what you need. You can then decide upon the best prescription, path, and people to help you with your grief journey.

**Survivor Strategies:**

Think: When was the last time you were honest about what's on your mind? How much focus have you put into your own needs? What can you do to ensure your needs are met?

Do: Decide what you'll do to give yourself the time, attention, and space to navigate the grieving process (i.e. ways to be "self-caretaking"), then, recruit a Supporter to make this journey easier for you.

**Supporter Strategies**:

Think: How can you encourage the Survivor to focus on his needs? How can you create an environment that encourages honesty and openness?

Do: Locate tools or assistance that will help the Survivor in this area (a list of these resources can be found on our Web site at www.2Grieve2Gether.org).

**Your Reflections**:

What's on your mind and in your heart after reading this entry and pondering the questions? In light of this, what will you do?

# CHAPTER 4

# KNOWING WHAT TO SAY

*November 26, 2009, written five months after Ralph's death*

GOOD Morning Baby,

Boy do I miss you! You'll be proud to know we made it through Thanksgiving. There was lots of laughter and love at the dinner table. As we began to eat, I had some flashbacks to last year and you sitting beside me at the table. This year, I thought about making everyone stop and have a moment of silence in honor of you. But, we didn't need to do that, because you were there, and we did honor you in our own way. You were on everyone's minds. Even as we grieve together, there's still awkwardness among us about what to say and when. I think it's funny that we said nothing and it was okay, yet I'm often mad at other people who say nothing to me about your passing. What a contradiction!

As I looked around the table, I wondered who would be missing next year. Life can be so painful. At the same time, the boys and I laughed a lot together yesterday. I knew that would please you. They are such wonderful tributes to you. I talk to them about you all the time, because we have such beautiful memories, and because I want you to be alive forever in their minds.

You've left these young men in my care, and I ask you to help me from time to time. I relied on you so much to provide me with guidance, balance, realism, and everything else it takes to raise young men. I try really hard to remember all you taught me and to honor your philosophy on raising them. As they become men, I am so lost about how to make the right decisions. But, I pray for divine insight and guidance. I read something the other day about allowing God to be your husband. I need to do that, because I'm ill-prepared for the job I'm now supposed to do alone. In fact, I can't do it alone!

Today Malcolm is having friends over and a million other things are going on. So, I guess I'll get myself together. As I do so, I want you to know that although I talk to you in my mind throughout each day, it feels good to formally write a letter to you each morning. It makes me feel a lot better, especially as I awake each day and feel the heaviness of "The Great Sadness" (remember *The Shack*). It feels good to express my thoughts to you. That's yet another thing to be thankful for!

**My Reflections**:

> Reading this entry makes me chuckle, because it's remarkable that a family that's been through so much loss would ever struggle with what to say to one another; yet that's what happened to us! It would be wonderful if we always knew exactly what to say or how to act. However, that's often not true. Survivors may get frustrated or hurt, because those around them don't know the right words or deeds that will help them heal. Yet sometimes Survivors don't know what to say or share with each other. And, if asked, Survivors may struggle with what they want and need to hear from others. Perhaps realizing this fact will give Survivors empathy toward Supporters and others who try to reach out to them.

**Survivor Strategies**:

> Think: What do you want people to say to you? What do you want people to do for or with you? What frustrations have you experienced when it comes to others reaching out?

Do: Determine the most effective (and comfortable) way to communicate your needs to potential Supporters, and then do it.

**Supporter Strategies**:

Think: How are you doing when it comes to communicating with the Survivor? How have you broken down any barriers that exist?

Do: Assist and encourage others to successfully communicate with the Survivor (and do the same yourself).

**Your Reflections**:

What's on your mind and in your heart after reading this entry and pondering the questions? In light of this, what will you do?

# CHAPTER 5

# ADDRESSING UNANSWERED QUESTIONS

*November 27, 2009, written five months after Ralph's death*

**D**EAR God,

I am boiling mad and hurt! In fact, I'm overwhelmed with tears of anger and sadness! Ralph and I both knew that I was not equipped to raise these boys alone. Ralph always said that it's difficult for a woman to teach a boy to be a man. He was able to reason with our sons, yet remain firm in his stance. So, why would you take Ralph away from us at the time when our family needed him the most? These boys are testing me in ways they would have never tested their dad. And they need guidance from their father, a man who was the best role model for them.

I need you to help me understand why I'm constantly dealing with pain and loss. First you take my mom when I'm in the middle of my child bearing and child rearing years, and you leave me without the person who helped me to make sense of motherhood and marriage. Then, you take my baby right after we felt we had truly been blessed with this unexpected miracle that brought new joy into our lives. Isaiah's death left a huge and never-to-be-filled hole in our family! When Aunt Flora tried to fill a gap in my life by being a friend and maternal influence, you took her away, making it hard for me to reach out to other older women, because you might take them from me too.

Now, when my boys need something I can never give them, you snatch away their father. You leave me alone to keep them from bad decisions. You leave me alone to figure out how I'm going to pay for college for three sons. You leave me alone to determine how to prepare them for sex, drugs, and all the other influences that can lure young men from the right path. You leave me alone to cry in my bed and wonder what I ever did to deserve all of this pain and heartache.

I just don't understand! Every day I see people who mock you, yet get blessed with easy lives, riches, and much more. Year after year, I find myself getting angrier and angrier. It doesn't come out against you. I talk about my love for you and the grace you've shown me, and I really mean it. But then, when the driver in front of me goes too slowly or the clerk at the store is a little dismissive, I have an angry reaction that far outweighs what was done to me. Now I realize it's not that person I'm mad at. It's you who I'm furious with! Worse still, there's no outlet for that. The world sees me as a bad person if I question God, and I feel I could be punished further if I admit how I really feel at times. But, I need to get it out and tell you that I am upset, hurt, and confused. I need to ask you the questions that are in my heart and mind. After all, how do I get answers if I never question anything?

Right now, I feel that until someone comes into my life and helps me to resolve the contradictions I sometimes feel about the love you're supposed to have for me and the constant losses that don't come close to making me feel loved, that anger will continue to fester beneath the surface. And I will continue to explode at drivers, coworkers, and others. My back, neck, and headache pain will continue to ravage my body, and my mind will continue to be overwhelmed from time to time with unimaginable and inconsolable sadness and depression.

I do not want to be mad at you, but unfortunately I am. While I can truthfully say that I continue to love you with all my heart despite everything that has happened, I can also say that I do not understand you, nor do I fully understand how you feel about me. I pray that one day I will, and in doing so, I'll be able to let go of this hurt and pain. I also pray that someone will fulfill Ralph's role and possess his best attributes so my sons don't have to suffer also. For now, I just pray that I can make it through tonight with this sore heart, throbbing head, swollen eyes, and exhausted mind. Good night.

**My Reflections**:

> I am struck by the raw honesty that escaped onto the pages of this entry. I've rarely admitted my anger at God for leaving me with all of these unanswered questions. That's because I didn't want people to judge me and see me as someone without faith.

> Ralph and I both felt tremendous pain after Isaiah died, and a lot of it was caused by all the questions we had for God. I still remember two wise Christian women visiting us and telling us it was okay to question God. While they couldn't guarantee us that we'd get answers in this lifetime, they assured us that questioning God meant that we were still talking to Him and that ongoing dialogue would allow us to have a closer relationship with Him.

> Sometimes Survivors suppress grief, anger, and questions, especially relevant to their deceased loved one or God. While this may seem helpful or prudent in the moment, it's rarely a good idea if it results in unresolved issues. Anger and unanswered and unsettling questions are a few of the reasons for Survivors to seek professional help with their grief. Such help allows them to release what's inside, process what they're feeling, and find effective strategies for the future.

**Survivor Strategies**:

> Think: Do you have any unanswered questions as a result of your loss? How are these questions affecting you mentally and physically? How are you handling your anger?

Do: Make a list of any unresolved questions and/or issues you have with anger. Then, find a resource to help you address those areas as soon as possible.

**Supporter Strategies**:

Think: Have you noticed the Survivor struggling with any unaddressed issues? Has the Survivor expressed any questions for God or their deceased loved one?

Do: Ask the Survivor to share the range of emotions she's feeling. If she mentions anger, find and share resources on anger and grief.

**Your Reflections**:

What's on your mind and in your heart after reading this entry and pondering the questions? In light of this, what will you do?

# Chapter 6

# Letting Go of Dreams

*November 27, 2009, written four years after Isaiah's death*

Dear Isaiah,

Today, you were on my mind and in my spirit. Perhaps it's because I just read the letters I wrote after you died and realized how emotional I was back then. In some ways, things haven't changed, because I'm still pretty emotional now. I keep thinking about the fact that you are now with your dad and wonder what that's like. I think about death way too much these days, but I guess that's natural because of the many tragedies that have hit this family.

I know that your father is finally at peace, especially because he's with you. At the same time, that's a realization I had to come to on my own, and I've been super annoyed by all the people who tried to push that thought on me. I know they just wanted to be kind and comforting; I just wasn't ready to hear it, and it needed to be my own conclusion, not someone else's.

Isaiah, as much as I'm comforted, it still doesn't stop me from missing you and wondering about what could (and should) have been. I've been thinking about what you would look like and what kind of personality you'd have. Would you be a mama's boy? I had so many hopes and dreams for your life. Like your brothers, I expected you to do wonderful things in this world and to be my pride and joy. I imagined you in school, at your high school and college graduations, starting a career, contributing to the community, having your own family, and living a long and fulfilling life. There was no limit to all you would accomplish.

So, as your mother, how do I deal with the reality that none of that will ever happen? How do I ever fill the hole in my heart that can only be occupied by you, my special little angel? Isaiah, I get sad when I think about the fact that many have already forgotten that you were here and far more will never know that you graced this earth. And so, my baby, I need to constantly acknowledge that you were (and always will be) a huge part of me and this family.

While I am comforted by the thought of you being safe in heaven, I still cry and long for you to rest in my arms. Yet, I'm relieved that you were spared the pain of experiencing the death of your father on this side of life, and I know that you are in the arms of both your father by birth and your Father by grace. Sweetie, I know we will all be reunited one day. But, until then, know that my periodic bouts of sadness about your death are also offset by intense feelings of joy as I remember all of the special moments we had together. It's hard to believe someone could bring such joy in only five months, but you did, little Isaiah. For that, I will always be grateful!

**My Reflections**:

> This reminds me of the reality that when someone dies, especially your child, you don't just lose who that person was at the time of their death or what they meant to you in the past. You also lose the hopes and dreams you had for that person's life. Often, you've imagined a perfect life with wonderful outcomes. As such, it's devastating when that view of perfection is robbed from us. What's also taken from us is the role that person did (and would have) played in our lives. And so, appropriately, there is a hole left behind in the space that person would have occupied in our hearts. As a result, there is emotional and mental anguish, along with a sense of disorientation that may plague us

at the time of the loss and then revisit us from time to time in the years to come. Having that pain resurge does not mean we are not healing. It just means that the loss will always be with us and may affect us at unexpected times. When this happens, we can work our way through pain either by self-reflection or by reaching out to others who can assist us.

**Survivor Strategies:**

Think: What is the future that you had imagined with your loved one who died? How are you dealing with the fact that those dreams will never be realized with that person? Are there more effective ways to deal with it in the future?

Do: To track your progress and analyze your feelings, keep a journal of your thoughts and feelings related to your loss and your life, along with your ideas and plans for dealing with those thoughts and feelings.

**Supporter Strategies:**

Think: What "dreams of the future" do you think the Survivor is mourning? How might you help the Survivor when she has surges of pain related to what she's lost from the past, present, and future?

Do: Give the Survivor a journal or some other tool for reflection.

**Your Reflections:**

What's on your mind and in your heart after reading this entry and pondering the questions? In light of this, what will you do?

# CHAPTER 7

# EVALUATING EARLY LOSS EXPERIENCES

*November 28, 2009, written twenty-six years after my grandmother's death*

**D**EAR Grandmom,

I felt like I spent today with you. That's because ten of us made the trip to New Jersey to see your only living sister. It was nice, because the children of each of your three deceased daughters were represented. We had such a great time as we talked about growing up and family memories. When I looked at and listened to your sister, my great aunt, it was as if you were still alive. The two of you look, sound, and think so much alike. That's why I left there with thoughts of you and am writing to you now. It's almost mindboggling when I think about the fact that you passed away almost thirty years ago, yet tears still come to my eyes as I reflect on the impact your death had on me.

You passed away from heart failure at the hospital, just after having your second leg amputated because of diabetes. For me, it was so unexpected. I was only sixteen and loved you with all of my heart. Each year, when I came home from the first day of school, you would be waiting to ask about all the details of how my day went. The year you died, I entered my senior year and felt sadness overcome me when I came home that first day of school, and there was no one to tell about my day. I remember feeling extremely depressed that year, and I now relate that to you leaving me. Unfortunately, people didn't really talk much about grief back then. While I remember my mother telling me that you never get over the death of your mother (I later found out how right she was), we never really discussed my feelings or coping skills.

So, all these years later, I'm left to analyze the impact and work through the scars. While I think I've been far more intentional with my kids, this makes me realize that I probably need to engage them more. I know they were getting accustomed to coming home and having their dad there waiting for them as he was off on disability before he died. Malcolm even talks about how they got to know one another so much better during that time. I know now that I need to keep engaging them in discussions, thinking about holes they might have because he's gone, and finding ways to support and love them through this. Wow, Grandmom, here you are still helping me twenty-seven years later. Thank you for that and for always being there for me. I love you now and forever!

**My Reflections**:

> I smile when I think about what an important role my grand-mother (and all of my grandparents) played in my life. No wonder her death had such an incredible impact on me. Our first experiences with loss can be pretty devastating and confusing. If it occurs when we're very young, we may not have the tools or be given the support to completely address and deal with our emotions and questions. How you get through it depends on whether your family talks about things such as death, whether there's any dysfunction going on, whether they have the tools and coping skills to address the issue, whether they seek outside assistance, and a million other factors.

> In a perfect world, everything you deal with would be handled in the best way for you. However, we know that's not the case.

If we did have significant help dealing with early losses, we can learn from that, use that information to better handle other deaths, and share our experiences and knowledge with others. However, if we didn't have help and/or if the issue was never discussed or addressed, we can still learn from an honest assessment of what was missing, what was needed, and what you think should have been done differently. That knowledge can then be applied in the future so that the grief experience is a little less difficult and a little more manageable. This doesn't mean the loss won't still be devastating and confusing. It just means that you may be able to navigate your grief journey a little better than before.

**Survivor Strategies**:

Think: What were your first experiences with loss? How did you cope? How has it impacted you?

Do: Write down what you learned from your first experiences with loss, and as a result, determine what you can do the same or differently now or in the future.

**Supporter Strategies**:

Think: Is this the first loss the Survivor has experienced? Have there been multiple losses? How should you adjust your approach with the Survivor based on his experience (or inexperience) with death and grieving?

Do: Obtain a resource that takes into consideration the Survivor's level of experience and coping skills with loss.

**Your Reflections**:

> What's on your mind and in your heart after reading this entry and pondering the questions? In light of this, what will you do?

# CHAPTER 8

# RESENTING THOSE
# WHO AREN'T THERE

*November 28, 2009, written five months after Ralph's death*

HEY Ralph,

You are always on my mind! I feel like I'm thinking of and talking to you all the time. Over the last few days, I keep running into people who say they were thinking about us over the holidays. It's still hard sometimes for me to hear that. I wonder if that's just what they say because they have nothing else to say. Do they say it because they feel guilty that they haven't reached out or called us at all? Did they mean to reach out but just never got around to it? All those people who were at the funeral saying "I'm going to be there for you" haven't been there. But, I knew that would be the case already. So why am I so angry about that?

I know God doesn't give me who or what I want, but instead who or what I need. But still, I'm not sure about who's being genuine around me and who's not. That's the role you played. You were able to decipher that for me. And, you were quick to tell me when you thought someone wasn't sincere. Now, I'm on my own and confused. I guess I should just air on the side of being more trusting and forgiving. I can hear you whispering that in my ear. In fact, I know you're saying, "Don't be like me, because what I always loved about you was that you trusted people more than I did."

So, I'll try to be less suspicious. If people are being disingenuous, that's on them. In fact, my prayer is that I stop worrying about what's not important (like who wasn't there). What's significant is that we're continuing to move forward each day. Despite our pain, despite our loneliness, despite our sadness, we're still making it. I hope you're proud of that!

**My Reflections**:

> This entry reflects an issue that's continued to plague me over the years: being sensitive about whether people reach out. What I know is that it's natural for people to feel deeply for a Survivor once they hear the bad news that their loved one has died. As they rush to comfort and assist the Survivor in those early days, especially before and during the funeral, they often have a sincere desire to share soothing words with the person who is hurting. That includes offers that they'll be there in the days to come. However, in the days, weeks and months following the funeral, their busy lives naturally go on. And so, as much as they thought they'd be there for the Survivor, other things often take priority and before long a significant amount of time may have passed without them being there as they had promised. This usually doesn't involve conspiracy or callousness; it's just the reality of people's crazy, hectic lives.

> At the same time, there are those who will be there as promised. There will also be those you never expected to be there, but who reach out anyway. Oftentimes, it can be much healthier to focus more on what you have rather than what you want. That change in perspective can make all the difference.

**Survivor Strategies**:

Think: What's on your mind most these days? How much time have you spent thinking about those people who haven't been there for you? Who has been there for you?

Do: Identify someone who you really need but who hasn't been there for you; if appropriate, find a way to constructively express your needs to that person. In addition, think about a Supporter who's gone above and beyond to be there for you and thank him or her for that effort.

**Supporter Strategies**:

Think: In what ways have you been there for the Survivor? Is there anything else you'd like to do to help the Survivor? What help or support do you need as you help the Survivor?

Do: Find a way to help others understand how they can support the Survivor.

**Your Reflections**:

What's on your mind and in your heart after reading this entry and pondering the questions? In light of this, what will you do?

# CHAPTER 9

# BEING A WALKING CONTRADICTION

*November 30, 2009, written five months after Ralph's death*

Dear Ralph,

Sorry that I didn't write to you yesterday. I slept a little late and then rushed to join William at church since he was ushering. The speaker said a few things that stuck with me. Specifically, she talked about the need to let our children know they are valued and to talk to them more about what's going on in their lives. I want to work on both areas. I feel like I need to be a mom and dad to our kids right now, and that because of my own grief I've sometimes disregarded my duties with them. That's nothing new, though, because there were times in the past when I put things like work and friends before my family. You used to get on me about that, and I'm sad that I was too hard headed to see and change that before you died. If I could go back in time, I would do so many things differently (at least I hope I would). Anyway, I've prayed for help in doing an "about face" in this area and pouring more time and love into our children. They need me and I need them!

On another matter, for the last couple days I've been thinking about something I wanted to share with you. Despite Mom having died fourteen years ago, I still feel a tinge of jealousy when I'm out and I see mothers and daughters together. Because of the loss of our son, Isaiah, it's still difficult for me to share someone else's happiness as they celebrate the birth of a child (I still can't attend baby showers). In fact, I sometimes still feel resentment when I see someone with a five-month-old baby, and I wonder why she got to keep her child and we didn't. In our extended family, when others talk about something they did with another aunt, I feel myself getting angry thinking about Aunt Flora being killed two years ago and the fact that there's been no one who's filled the gap she left behind. Now, with you gone, I hurt when I see couples and families together. I feel a lot of loneliness when I think about you not being here to love me and the boys. Most of all, when I see people whose lives have been relatively untouched by loss and tragedy, I wonder why they're so special and we're not.

I know there are people who would tell me that instead of asking "why me," I should ask "why not me." However, I'm tired of being the person people look at and feel sorry for because I've been through so much. I'm tired of wondering whether there's some kind of curse on my family. I'm exhausted from pondering what we must have done wrong. Others will say I shouldn't think all those things, but what have those same people been through in their own lives? I don't want to be the modern day version of Job from the Bible, nor do I want my kids to have to suffer through more loss. When will all of this stop? When will happiness replace hurt? When will I stop being afraid of what tragedy awaits us around the corner? When will I stop resenting people because they don't know what to say to me, they don't know how to approach me, they haven't been through anything, or they forget that our family is in pain?

I know I am a walking contradiction! I want people to reach out to me and feel angry when they don't, yet sometimes I feel frustrated when they do. I feel sorry for myself when I think of all we've been through, yet I know that many in this world have suffered much more than me. I feel abandoned by God because of all this pain, yet know that I am truly loved by Him. I physically ache when I think of how much I miss all of you and want you back, yet I know that one day we'll be reunited, and that you are truly in a better place (although I resent people who find the need to tell me that).

Oh Ralph, I am such a basket case. Sometimes, I wish people didn't just see the strong exterior and instead could see that I am grieving and need their love and support now more than ever. That's yet another contradiction: I only show people the strong side, yet want them to know I'm not that strong and need their support. You were the only one who saw all my contradictions and quirks. You knew my real personality and not just the persona I project. And, you loved me in spite of all those things. So, what do I do now when no one's here to know and love me just as I am? Who do I turn to and how do I fill this void? I guess when I'm able to answer those questions, my love, some of this pain will go away. Until then, thank you for being there to listen, if only in my heart.

**My Reflections:**

> Boy was I a basket case! Actually, I still am! Reflecting on this journal entry makes me face my "demons" again and realize that I have to let people in so that they can see the real me. Have you ever heard the old adage that you can't judge a book by its cover? In this crazy and fast-paced world, people don't always have the time or energy to go beyond the cover of the book. And sometimes, they choose not to go beyond the cover, because they're afraid of what is really there and their possible inability to deal with that reality. So, when a potential Supporter sees a Survivor who constantly smiles or seems to be okay, they are relieved and may jump to the conclusion that everything is alright.

> The Survivor, in her pain, doesn't always go out of her way to correct these assumptions. And so, the Survivor doesn't share what's really going on and the person who could be a Supporter doesn't go deep enough to learn what the person really needs. Hence, a lack of communication and connection ensues. But this situation can easily be changed via a simple conversation or

a few genuine questions. This includes the Survivor taking the risk of opening up to others and the Supporter taking the time to dig a little deeper.

**Survivor Strategies**:

Think: Who knows how you're really doing? Who else would you like to know? What can you do now to let people in? What benefits would you gain from doing so?

Do: Take a risk and be honest the next time someone asks you how you're doing (do that with a few people, because everyone won't react in the way you need them to). When you find the person who reacts in a way that is helpful or nurturing, consider developing a deeper relationship with that person.

**Supporter Strategies**:

Think: How have you been able to go deeper with the Survivor? If the Survivor doesn't tend to share, what things can you do to help him express his feelings? Also, how are you really doing?

Do: Tell someone how you're really doing and communicate what you need from that person.

**Your Reflections**:

What's on your mind and in your heart after reading this entry and pondering the questions? In light of this, what will you do?

# CHAPTER 10

# BALANCING OUR MEMORIES

*December 2, 2009, written six months after Ralph's death*

D EAR Ralph,

It's four o'clock in the morning, and I've just been awakened by an unsettling dream about you. In the dream, it was me, you, and the kids. Other people were also there. In the dream, you did something that was a little mean and really embarrassed me. When I awakened, it made me think. During the last six months, I've been placing you in this god-like role and thought of you only as this perfect man. At the same time, I've placed myself in the exact opposite role as this horrible wife. Just the other day, I found myself in tears thinking about you dying and about how many ways I had failed you. It was almost unbearable, and I remember asking for your forgiveness.

This morning, in the aftermath of that unsettling dream, I'm realizing that it's unfair to both of us for me to remember us as only the extremes. You were a wonderful man who loved me with all of your heart. You told me more than once that you would give your life for me, and I knew it was true. You also performed many acts of love for me, such as making sure my gas tank was full, coming to pick me up at night because you knew I wasn't good at driving after certain hours, and taking such good care of our children. More than that, I've read some of the notes you'd written down over the years. They further acknowledge the love you felt for me, and that really warms my heart.

At the same time, there were moments when you could be a real jerk! You could say or do things that would just crush my heart and/or my self-esteem. Sometimes, you would apologize later. Other times, you just wouldn't. I often said that we had this intense love/hate relationship that was a dream when it was good and a nightmare when it was bad! There were also times when I was a sweet, kind, and loving wife to you. I'm realizing this morning that I wasn't all bad. All those nights when I slept beside your hospital bed, it was out of love, nothing more and nothing less. I could go on, but the point is that I had both my good and bad moments too. Honey, I'm realizing this early morning that it serves no purpose for me to deify you and vilify myself. It just makes the grieving more intense and keeps me from moving forward.

I think that from this moment on, I'll try to remember both the good and bad about our relationship and the things we did, and then I'll remember to be thankful for both! Thank God that we were imperfect people with an imperfect relationship! That made it real, intense, exciting, and even more. It also gave our sons a realistic picture of the ups, downs, and ultimate beauty of a real relationship. Believe it or not, I do miss the good and the bad. In fact, I would take nothing but the bad if I could have you back for just one moment to tell you how much I love and appreciate you. While that's not possible for now, I hope that this letter will serve that purpose. Thank you, my love.

**My Reflections**:

This realization was a turning point for me. At the same time, it's a lesson I have to continually relearn, because it's natural for our memories to get stuck in certain ruts. Isn't it funny what our minds will focus on? Our memories of certain people or events can be totally skewed by what's going on at the current moment. For instance, if someone does something nice for you and you're looking at them in a favorable light at the moment, your recollection of past interactions would most likely be focused on all the good things that happened. Similarly, if someone makes you mad, you may only see the bad.

Grief can have the same outcome. A Survivor who's upset at a loved one for dying may focus primarily on negative memories. A Survivor who believes it is poor manners to "speak ill of the dead" may think it's improper to reflect on the bad deeds attributed to a deceased love one. Another example would be a Survivor who feels guilt over the death of his loved one. He may see that guilt manifest itself via constant thoughts of all the ways the Survivor was the "bad guy" while the loved one was "the good guy" in their relationship. Rarely is any relationship that extreme. Reality is usually some place in the middle, and healing may often be found when the Survivor can realistically acknowledge his full range of memories of the loved one.

**Survivor Strategies**:

Think: How are you acknowledging both the highs and lows of your relationship with the person who has died? Is there anything that keeps you from doing so? If that's the case, how can you get past this so you can better deal with reality?

Do: Find someone who's trustworthy and a great listener, and then share both good and bad memories with that person.

**Supporter Strategies**:

Think: Are there ways you can encourage the Survivor to open up? How can you assure her that she is safe in sharing with you or another trusted friend?

Do: Find a helpful tool or resource that allows the Survivor to process her memories and feelings.

**Your Reflections**:

What's on your mind and in your heart after reading this entry and pondering the questions? In light of this, what will you do?

# CHAPTER 11

# REPLACING KEY ROLES

*December 3, 2009, written fourteen years after Mom's death*

D EAR Mom,

Today I feel overwhelmed, because I have so much I need to accomplish. For the longest time you were the main person who I'd ask for help. Not only that, you were the person who I spent much of my time with and who knew all my secrets, fears, faults, and strengths. You showed me a mother's unconditional love and acceptance. I know that not all mothers and daughters have the same relationship as we did. You were truly my best friend, and I'm thankful for that. Now that you're gone, it's hard to allow others to play some of the roles you played in my life. I want *you* to help me, not other people! Yes, I'm feeling sorry for myself! Why can't you be here?

Mom, you had a way of looking at me and knowing that I was stressed. After Tre was born, there were so many times when you'd insist on taking him for the night so I could have some relief (you said your mom had done the same thing for you). On top of that, I think of the many times I came to you first with a problem so you could listen and provide me with no-nonsense advice. I reflect on all the times we went shopping as a way to relax and have fun. It's amazing that we hardly spent any money; we just had fun window shopping and talking. I remember all the times we went out to dinner to laugh and catch up. Just as often, you'd invite us to your house for Sunday dinners and holidays. Most of all, I recall you telling me what I needed to hear and not what I wanted to hear (actually I remember you "kicking me in the butt" quite a few times). Doing all those things together (along with knowing that you had loved me from the moment you knew I was growing in your stomach) made it easy for me to ask you for the world. You made me feel loved, included, and taken care of!

All these years later, it's apparent that you could never be replaced. No one could ever do all that you did for me (nor would it feel the same). It would also be unfair to place that kind of burden on someone else. I guess all I can do now is hold on to my memories while being appreciative that I have such good memories to cherish. Right now, I can hear you whispering in my ear to please allow other people in. Actually, you'd probably be a little more forceful, telling me something like, "Denise, stop being a big old baby; get over yourself, and let people help you." I know you're right. I also know that there are various people, like dad and Alice [my stepmother], who can (and have) taken on a small piece of what you did for me. I guess I should be happy that I at least have that! In reality, I am. I just need to be reminded of that fact every now and then. For now, I think that tomorrow I'll pick up the phone and get a little help with the things that are overwhelming me. Good night, Mom!

**My Reflections:**

> This journal entry makes me smile because it represents the written version of what happens in my head all the time! Because my mother played such vital and necessary roles in my life, I frequently catch myself talking to her and hearing her firm (but loving) advice. I still need her! Often, a deceased loved one has played key roles in a Survivor's life. Whether they served as confidante, companion, collaborator, or in another capacity, the Survivor obviously needed or desired having someone play that role in their life. The question then becomes: what do you when the person who fulfilled a key role is gone? How do you replace that role? Keep in mind that the question is not about

how you replace that person because a person can never truly be replaced. However, it may be necessary to have someone else (or a group of people) serve in the role(s) that your loved one played. Jobs like babysitter, exercise partner, event planner, and spiritual advisor are just a few examples of roles you may still need in your life. Finding "surrogates" is not a sign of weakness nor does it diminish your loved one. It simply acknowledges that life goes on and so must the Survivor.

**Survivor Strategies**:

Think: What are a few key roles that the deceased person played in your life? Which of these roles do you still need or want in your life?

Do: Seek and find people to help you with a few of the key roles you still need in your life.

**Supporter Strategies**:

Think: What key roles did the deceased person play in the Survivor's life? Is there any role that the Survivor would want you to assume?

Do: Ask the Survivor about the key roles the loved one played and how you could help with those roles.

**Your Reflections**:

What's on your mind and in your heart after reading this entry and pondering the questions? In light of this, what will you do?

# CHAPTER 12

# PLEASING PEOPLE

*December 5, 2009, written six months after Ralph's death*

D EAR Ralph,

Today I went to a Christmas party. It didn't go well. The reason is familiar: I put the wishes of others before my own needs and it had a predictable outcome! You see, babe, an acquaintance invited a group of people to his house, and I decided not to go, because the last time this group got together, you were there. The thought of you not being there this time made me unbelievably sad. Also, I knew it would be nothing but couples, and I'm no longer part of a couple. Finally, with the Christmas season upon us, I figured I might be a little emotional. Anyway, after I declined, the host asked me why I wasn't coming. I gave him the aforementioned reasons, but he said he'd really appreciate it if I would be there. So, I reluctantly agreed to attend.

I think other people have the best intentions; they just don't always understand the grieving process. He probably insisted because he wanted to make sure I felt included or that I wasn't alone. Who knows? In any case, on the way to the party, I started to cry. I eventually had to pull over because I was so overwhelmed. I then called my friend Melanie, a fellow widow, and she talked me through it. She first encouraged me to go back home. However, because I'm always overly concerned about disappointing people, I told her that I had to attend. She then advised me not to stay very long and to find a friendly face that could help me to get out of there quickly if I needed to. I got myself together and entered the gathering. Unfortunately, as soon as I saw a couple of familiar faces, I felt myself getting emotional again. Only minutes after I gave the host my coat, I knew I had to get out of there. So, I asked a friendly face to retrieve my coat for me. As I made my way back to the door, the tears really came and a couple people entering the party saw me. You know how I try so hard to be professional and to keep my personal life to myself, so I'm sure you can imagine how devastated and embarrassed I was. Ralph, why did I go when I already knew it would be hard? I knew that I would miss you too much. I knew that the familiar thoughts about "why me" and "why not someone else" would come up. But, as always, I did what others wanted me to do and disregarded my own heart and instincts. Why do I do that? Why am I such a people pleaser? In addition, why didn't they know this would be too difficult? Think about it; it's only been six months!

After I left, I made separate calls to Tia [my sister] and Joy [my cousin]. As I spilled my guts and my insecurities, between a heavy dose of sobs and sniffles, they allowed me to unload and they shared my burden. I am so grateful to have them. At the same time, I wish I still had you here physically. You were always here to listen as I told you about hurts and disappointments (like today's party and the fact that none of the guests called to check on me). Writing you this letter is okay, because I am able to get some of my feelings out, but it's a weak substitution. I want you, and tonight's ordeal reminded me that I'm still angry that you were taken away from us. We didn't even get to say "goodbye." You didn't even get to make it to fifty, the same thing that happened with my mom. Ralph, tonight I do not feel like rationalizing or focusing only on the positive. Tonight I feel like just wallowing, and I'm okay with that right now. In fact, I think I deserve a pity party once in a while. And so, as I end this letter, I'm going to lay in our bed, think about you, weep for a little while longer, and get out some pent up emotions. Hopefully, I'll feel a lot better in the morning. Goodnight.

## My Reflections:

What stands out to me about this entry is the positive role Supporters have played in my journey. That may seem like an odd statement because the entry involves me lamenting about people not being sensitive to my pain. But, as I look at what occurred, I am struck by the strong support from my friend, cousin, and sister, because without them the situation would have been more disastrous! Reflecting on the event also allows me to see my own actions, as well as the actions of the others involved, in a totally different light. I now realize that my strong desire to please others resulted in me saying yes to something I intuitively knew wasn't good for me. Then, when it didn't go well, I pointed fingers. And even though the hosts and guests never knew how I felt, I continued to be hurt by what I assumed was their insensitivity. Unfortunately, when a Survivor and those she interacts with do not fully communicate with one another, miscommunications and hurtful interactions may occur. So, how can we avoid this? A simple solution is for the Survivor to share her thoughts. If someone asks a Survivor to do something she doesn't feel comfortable with, the Survivor may want to have a candid conversation about why it's not a good idea. The Survivor may also decline and tell the person that she will explain more later (and do so when the Survivor has the mental and physical energy to address the issue in more detail). Sometimes, you won't be able to avoid miscues and friction. If that happens, the key is to talk about what happened whenever prudent. Finally, it's also helpful for Survivors to be candid with themselves. This could merely be an internal acknowledgement of both your positive and negative feelings.

**Survivor Strategies**:

Think: What do you need to candidly communicate to others? What's keeping you from doing so? How could others benefit from knowing what you really feel? How would you benefit from sharing your true emotions and thoughts?

Do: The next time someone asks you to do something, tell them you'll think about it and get back to them. Carefully consider all of the pros and cons before answering.

**Supporter Strategies**:

Think: How do you think the Survivor is doing? Is there anything you can do to help the Survivor be more candid with you or others? How are you doing?

Do: Encourage those who want to help to find resources such as those listed on www.2Grieve 2Gether.org.

**Your Reflections**:

What's on your mind and in your heart after reading this entry and pondering the questions? In light of this, what will you do?

# CHAPTER 13

# HAVING A COMPANION IN ADVERSITY

*December 15, 2009, written six months after Ralph's death*

D EAR Ralph,

Today I had a really good conversation with my friend Hope. We talked about you and her husband, the sadness we each feel as a result of both of you passing away, and how we both missed our partners. We also talked about how much we each relied on you guys as our sounding boards and confidants. Right now, we're both trying to figure out who we are as people and how to make decisions on our own. In doing so, we're trying to do a better job of living Christ-centered lives where we depend on God for guidance. What's interesting is that when you and her husband were here with us physically, we had an audible voice to answer our questions and to lead us. Now, the necessary transition involves learning to trust in answers that come from within. After the conversation, I realized that it meant that one day I'll probably write and talk more to God than I do to you. I'm not sure how I feel about that. I guess if it feels natural and right, I'll do it.

Hope and I both feel thankful for our friendship. I still marvel at the fact that she and I never knew one another before we were connected by the fact that our husbands had died within two weeks of one another. Despite me being in Maryland and her living in Florida, and later

Georgia, we have such a close friendship that I couldn't imagine making it through this without her. Most of all, we're both growing spiritually, rather than turning to negative forces to get us through this difficult time. While we wish we would have never been linked in the way that we are, we're both grateful for the wonderful men we married and the companionship we've found with each other. I know you're happy about that.

Ralph Brown, I love you! I might be going crazy, but I thank you for listening to my musings in these letters. I really feel you can hear me. It helps to get out my thoughts and feelings. There's something to be said for not holding everything in and being able to release what's inside without feeling judged. Thank you for giving me that. Goodnight baby.

**My Reflections**:

This warms my heart, because it embodies the title of this book. My friend and I are two women grieving together, and as a result of helping one another, we are both stronger. When we go through adversity, we do have a choice. We can allow the bad things that happen to permanently diminish and weaken us or we can allow hardships and pain to refine and strengthen us. The key is knowing that while it isn't as easy as it sounds, it is possible.

Recovering from the death of a loved one involves an ongoing process of evaluation and working through one's thoughts and emotions. Doing so by finding someone with whom you can share the journey can allow you to slowly release your feelings and the pain you're experiencing. Think about a volcano. It eventually erupts after an overwhelming amount of pressure builds inside of it. Such an eruption can be avoided via the slow release of that pressure. It is important for a Survivor not to be alone on the grief journey, but instead to be supported by people and resources that allow them to experience a gradual discharge of pressure. That shared experience is truly powerful for both the Survivor and the Supporter!

**Survivor Strategies**:

Think: What are you doing to release your pain? How has your behavior and relationships been impacted by your grief? Who and what are you turning to now? Who and what should you turn to in order to progress in the right direction?

Do: Assess where you are emotionally and determine whether you need additional help (including friends, family, a therapist or support group) to assist you. Then make it happen.

**Supporter Strategies**:

Think: What have you observed about the Survivor's behavior? Do you think he needs additional support? Where can you find resources to assist the Survivor? What help do you need in dealing with your own grief and/or supporting the Survivor?

Do: Initiate a conversation with the Survivor if you think he needs additional support. In addition, find help for yourself if you need it.

**Your Reflections**:

What's on your mind and in your heart after reading this entry and pondering the questions? In light of this, what will you do?

# CHAPTER 14

# PRACTICING GRATITUDE

*December 22, 2009, written six months after Ralph's death*

D EAR Ralph,

This week, we had 22 inches of snow! The first day, I went out to shovel by myself and then Tre joined me (Malcolm was in the basement playing video games and William stayed overnight with a friend). The second day, William went out on his own. Tre and Malcolm then joined him (after some prompting from their grandfather). I was so proud when I looked out the window and saw your three sons working together. Eventually, I felt sorry for them and joined the effort.

As we shoveled all that snow, I thought of you frequently and knew that you were looking down at us with pride. I'm guessing you were also wondering why we couldn't have been this industrious when you were alive. Boy did you take care of me! I never realized how spoiled I was! I can only imagine some of the conversations you had with yourself about my lack of help around (and especially outside) the house. It makes me laugh when I think of how much of a little princess I was (although you might have had a different word for me).

Anyway, whether it was shoveling the snow, taking care of the cars, working in the garage, or doing many of those activities that truly became an expression of your deep love for me and our family, I thank you for all you did. I love you not because you did stuff, but instead because I now see how much of a sacrifice it was for you and what a loving gesture it was. You gave our sons a great example of what a good man, a good husband, and a good father is. While I'll never expect perfection from them (after all, you have to admit you weren't perfect), I do look forward to them growing and developing into wonderful, caring men like their father. What a legacy! What a blessing!

**My Reflections**:

> I love seeing that every moment of my journey hasn't been painful, and that I have taken time out to reminisce about the good times even though I still felt the huge void left by my husband's absence. What's more interesting, though, is that from the moment we are born, we are in the process of dying. No matter who we are, each human being has a limited time on this earth. Our joys are limited, our pain is limited, and our time together is limited. Yet isn't it funny that we often live as if we have all the time in the world? So what if I don't tell you how much I appreciate you today; we'll always have tomorrow. Rationally, we all know that's not true, yet emotionally we don't deal with that truth for a variety of reasons. And so, we sometimes tend to take little things for granted. This includes failing to stop to think about all of the small ways we show love for one another. Instead, we may have a tendency to put a lot of energy into the ways we disappoint each other.
>
> Go to a mall, sit on a bench, and eavesdrop on a conversation or two. Many times, people are complaining about something someone didn't do or some conflict they're involved in. How often do you hear people who are praising a loved one's behavior? A wise person once said that we get what we focus on. Wouldn't it be great if we all focused primarily on the good stuff while a person was alive, rather than waiting until he dies? That small practice could make a huge difference in our lives. At the same time, when our loved ones die, it can also be helpful

to spend quality time reflecting on cherished memories of that person while also understanding that we will continue to make new memories with those remaining in our lives.

## Survivor Strategies:

Think: What are you focusing on now that your loved one has died? What did you focus on when that loved one was alive? Is there are difference? Would you have done anything differently if you could go back in time? What can you do differently with your loved ones who are still alive?

Do: Select two to three loved ones who are still in your life. Write a list of everything you love about them; then record anything about them that frustrates you. Now ask yourself if the frustrations would matter if the person died today. If not, let them go. If it would matter, determine what you can do to resolve the frustrations (then do it).

## Supporter Strategies:

Think: What is the status of your relationship with the Survivor? What do you appreciate about him? What frustrates you about him? In what ways can you strengthen the relationship with the Survivor?

Do: Spend some quality time with the Survivor where you focus on your relationship and not just the grief.

## Your Reflections:

What's on your mind and in your heart after reading this entry and pondering the questions? In light of this, what will you do?

# CHAPTER 15

# FACING FLASHBACKS

*December 23, 2009, written four years after Isaiah's death*

D<sup>EAR</sup> Isaiah,

Today was difficult, because for some reason I was overwhelmed with flashbacks of the day you died. I'm guessing that I'm feeling that extra pain because it's the Christmas season, and everything seems to be focused on the joy that little children find during this time. The only problem is that my child died and never got to experience the holiday. Not only that, but these flashbacks I'm having are filled with emotions that make me feel as if I'm living that horrible day all over again.

When I think back to that time, I remember sitting in my office and receiving a frantic call from your dad. At first, I couldn't understand him, but I finally made out the words, "Come home now. Isaiah stopped breathing." As I rushed the few short miles to our house, I wondered how a five-month old could stop breathing. I also bargained with God, repeating, "Please God, please God, just let Isaiah be okay." I can't even remember all the things I promised to change if you would just be alright. When I got home, there was an ambulance sitting out front. I rushed in and your distraught father was surrounded by police officers; none of this made sense. Your dad then managed to blurt out that he thought he took you to daycare that morning but apparently had forgotten and left you in the car. When he discovered you, he tried to revive you and called 911. Your dad, one of the strongest men I ever knew, was a wreck and something inside told me I had to be strong (for once) for both of us. Not long after, someone told us that you, our precious baby, didn't make it. A piece of me died when my mom passed away; a chunk of me died when you left this earth.

When they took us to the hospital and ushered us into a depressing little room, your grandmother and other family members were already there to be with us. Everyone was inconsolable. Eventually, they asked if we wanted to see you and, naturally, we needed to. No one should see such a tiny, precious body on a slab. You looked like a doll. I remember your dad cradling you while crying and apologizing. I finally had to make him put you down. We left the room and eventually the hospital. However, before we came home, we promised to support one another (and your brothers) through this horrible ordeal.

When I look back on the days after your death, it's as if we were all in such a daze. We lived from moment to moment as we tried to call people to let them know what happened, muster enough energy to make decisions, and support one another through a horrific tragedy. Added to that, we quickly found ourselves on the "other side" of the legal system, which chose to prosecute your dad for your death. Isaiah, your dad was, by far, one of the best fathers in the world. He simply had a horrible lapse in his memory because his routine changed, and he was distracted by rushing back home to donate our van to charity. It's hard to believe that trying to do something so good could have turned out so bad!

Your father loved all of you guys so much, and he was devastated by what happened. While dealing with the unbelievable pain of losing you, he also had to face prosecution for your death. In many ways, I understand why he had to go through that; they had to make sure there wasn't a criminal act involved, and that he was not intentionally negligent—which he was not. In the end, he was sentenced to community service and probation. No punishment from society could even come close to the way your dad punished himself for the rest of his life.

Isaiah, I feel like I'm finally explaining what happened to you, and for some reason, it feels necessary. Many people judged our family, and especially your father, because of what happened. You can't believe the horrible things some people said and wrote without ever knowing us personally. I want you to know that we all loved you so much. We all suffered greatly because of your death, and each of us would have easily given our lives in exchange for yours. I wonder if your dad has already told you all this; I'm sure he has. Anyway, it feels good to connect with you in this moment. I wonder what gifts I'd be spoiling you with if you were alive. I also can't help wondering why we sometimes spend more time appreciating the people who we've lost and not as much time appreciating those who are still with us. And so, with that thought, I'm going to take some time to appreciate those who are still with me on this earth. Now that's a Christmas gift! Good night, my little prince!

**My Reflections**:

> For some reason, I needed to document what unfolded the day that my son died. Perhaps it's because there will now be a record of that day from my perspective. Maybe it's because I never got the chance to have a final conversation with my son and needed to reconcile what happened. When someone dies, things are not always tied up in a nice, neat bow. So, what happens when someone dies suddenly and/or tragically with no opportunity for important discussions and explanations? How can a Survivor address unresolved issues? While the solutions may not be perfect, it is possible to use therapy, journaling, or another means to have an indirect conversation with your loved one. Finding an outlet for these thoughts can allow the Survivor to release pain, process grief, and make an effort to move forward.

**Survivor Strategies**:

> Think: Are there any issues that you were never able to resolve with your deceased loved one? How are those issues impacting you today? What will you do about it?

Do: Address any unresolved issues via journaling, therapy, or another outlet.

**Supporter Strategies**:

Think: In examining your conversations with the Survivor, are there any unresolved issues that you think could be impacting the Survivor? If so, what do you think would be the best way to broach those issues with the Survivor?

Do: Ask the Survivor if there are any issues that are greatly affecting him and, if so, help him to brainstorm ways to resolve the issues.

**Your Reflections**:

What's on your mind and in your heart after reading this entry and pondering the questions? In light of this, what will you do?

# CHAPTER 16

# MOURNING AS THE WORLD CELEBRATES

*December 25, 2009, written six months after Ralph's death*

DEAR Ralph,

It's 7:15 AM on Christmas morning. The last twenty-four hours have been such a roller coaster. Yesterday at about this time, your friend Doc called. He was at the cemetery putting flowers on your grave and wanted to stop by to deliver presents for the boys. When he arrived, he said he would be driving to the grave sites of his two sons next. For some reason, hearing him say that brought to my eyes a stream of tears that I just couldn't stop. I thought about the tragedy he's seen in his life, losing two sons and then you, his surrogate son. Sometimes, I feel like I'm the only one who's been through something, but then I remember that so many in this world are hurting.

Once he left, I drove to meet a friend for breakfast. For some reason, I cried the whole way. I ended up calling Alice [my stepmother] to say that I didn't think I'd be able to cook Christmas dinner this year. Last year was such a perfect Christmas with you helping me with the meal and your four sisters and their families attending. I feel like I should have known that when things are that perfect, something bad will happen. I should have known that it would be our last Christmas together. Maybe if I had known, I would have appreciated it even more. I remember that when your sisters were telling stories about you growing up I was not in the room because some of my friends had stopped by. You later said you were disappointed that I didn't hear the stories. Now I see why it was so important for me to be there, and I sincerely regret missing it. If only I could turn back the hands of time.

When I left breakfast yesterday, I called my sister and just hearing her voice made the tears come again. Being the supportive sister she is, she rushed right over. We then ended up going shopping for last-minute gifts for the boys. Unlike previous years, I hadn't done much shopping. The time we spent together was full of conversations, memories, and laughter; it was good for me. We planned to have a few friends come over in the evening, and I was really looking forward to doing something out of the ordinary like that. But, when I got home, it's like all the energy just left my body.

William asked me to make him some tomato soup. As simple as that was, I just couldn't do it. All I could do was sit in my chair; I couldn't even move. A couple friends called with words of support. However, I couldn't bring myself to answer the telephone to talk to them. I did have enough energy to call your sister Lynn (just in case I missed her on Christmas). She, along with your sisters Sue and Delores were in the car on their way to your oldest sister, Ann's house. I was glad that they'd all be together again. But, as soon as I heard Lynn's voice, the tears came again. I know they're all hurting too. I know Lynn could tell I was crying and that was definitely not what I wanted to happen. I don't want to be that person who brings everyone else down with my pain. Anyway, it was good talking to her. I do love your sisters and am grateful to have them as a connection to you. Tia (my sister) returned soon after, sensing something was wrong, and I still never left the chair. I told her that I was just tired. She asked me if I needed help wrapping the gifts for the kids, and I said no. That was always your job, and I told her that I might not wrap gifts this year. In fact, I hadn't even purchased wrapping paper. She tried to remind me that Malcolm was just twelve years old, but none of that mattered. As helpful as she was trying to be, there's no way for her to understand what was going on inside of me.

When she left, I moved to the bed and could not do anything else. I think it was a wave of depression that just took over my whole body. It was only 7:30 PM, and I apologized to the kids and told them they were on their own for dinner. But here's where the blessing comes in. At about 11:30 p.m., the phone rang. It is extremely unusual for anyone to call the house that late at night. However, I was semi-awake and answered. It was Aunt Karen on the other end. She told me she thinks about us all the time and wanted to see if we were okay. When I told her I was struggling a little, she asked me if I wanted to talk about it. We only talked for about ten minutes, yet it was unbelievable the impact it had on me. It was as if someone poured just enough energy and grace into me that I could lay my burdens aside for a minute and do something for our children.

As soon as I hung up, I went downstairs, found some bags for the gifts, dragged the presents from the closet, and sat down to make Christmas a little special for the boys. I am so thankful for those moments of clarity. Now, I need you to know that it was not like previous years. You know how I used to frustrate you by having each child's gifts wrapped in their own distinctive paper and making sure we arranged them so they would open them in a certain order. Boy was I a control freak!

This year, I used any bags I had and there was absolutely no method to my madness. And, you know what, it was okay. By about 1:00 a.m., I was able to get into bed, content that I had not let my pain rob our children of some sense of normalcy. Ralph, everyone talks about how strong I am. But, it's the kids who have to see and deal with my weakness. They are the ones who see me when I can't get out of bed or when I'm having sad days that I can't control. Why couldn't I have shielded them from this? Why couldn't I have made their lives easier instead of making them worry about me? Sometimes I wonder if I need counseling to help me through this. It's been six months, but sometimes it feels like it was just yesterday. I pray for the wisdom to make the right decisions.

Well, dear, my nose is running and my face is soaking wet as I write to you. I would give anything to be here in your arms right now. As that's not possible, I will hold you in my heart as I try to make this day normal for our three sons. At least, on this special day, I'm with them and you're with Isaiah, so today all of our children will be in the loving embrace of at least one of their parents. Thank you for all of the Christmases past and know that I look forward to the day when we will celebrate a heavenly Christmas together.

**My Reflections**:

It is not hard for me to remember the pain of that day. It's also not difficult to understand why Survivors sometimes feel as if they're in a bubble where they can see the world, but the world really can't see them, because no one truly sees the pain underneath the surface. Isn't it ironic to be hurting when the world is rejoicing? Whether it's Christmas, Hanukkah, Kwanzaa or some other celebration, holidays often involve jovial people who are in the mood to celebrate.

For a Survivor, however, the holidays can offer a stark reminder of what they've lost. This may include being overwhelmed with memories of past celebrations with their loved one and sadness over traditions that may forever be changed. Rarely does society stop to pause during the holidays to acknowledge those who are grieving. Instead, people may go about their merry ways while the Survivor struggles to make it through this period. Many times, the Survivor may mask the pain of the loss and the resentment they feel toward the rest of the world's happy demeanor.

It is okay to experience conflicted emotions. What can be harmful is suppressing one's feelings and not addressing the root of the problem. Dealing with these feelings may involve the Survivor finding outlets to express themselves, including Supporters who allow them to vent, explore their feelings, and establish new traditions. While the holidays may never again be the same, it is possible to eventually get to a place where they don't evoke as much pain and heartache. In fact, at some point the Survivor may even celebrate the holidays again, only this time it's as a new person who is sensitive to what the holiday really represents to someone who's had a loss.

**Survivor Strategies**:

Think: How are you feeling about the holidays? How will you overcome any struggles you may experience? What is the best way for a Supporter to assist you during this time?

Do: Find a least one person with whom you can share your emotions about holidays. Then take time to have a serious conversation in which you can process your feelings.

**Supporter Strategies**:

Think: How do you act and feel during the holidays? How might this demeanor impact the Survivor? How can you help the Survivor during this time?

Do: Have a candid conversation with the Survivor to see how you can best support her during the holidays.

**Your Reflections**:

What's on your mind and in your heart after reading this entry and pondering the questions? In light of this, what will you do?

# CHAPTER 17

# EXPERIENCING PEACE IN THE VALLEY

*December 25, 2009, written six months after Ralph's death*

H EY Babe,

There are only fifteen minutes left until Christmas is over. Before this day ends, I just wanted to let you know that we made it through! Christmas definitely wasn't the same without you. However, there was lots of laughter and love. I know you had to be looking down on us with pride! I am amazed at the resiliency of our boys and am thankful that they are one of my reasons to keep going. They are such loving and considerate children (at times … smile)!

After dinner, they presented me with a digital frame that included family pictures from over the years. How special! It even included photos of us opening the presents today. I sat it beside my bed so I could reflect on my many memories. Tomorrow, we're going away for a couple days of shopping. We'll be staying in a hotel and doing activities such as ice skating as one way for us to establish new traditions. We're all looking forward to it. Well, my love, I need my sleep. Tonight, I pray, that you'll be waiting for me in my dreams so that we can celebrate this day together. I love you!

**My Reflections**:

I am thankful for the respite my family was able to find on that special day. It makes me think of the Thomas Dorsey song, "There Will Be Peace in the Valley," because it contains so much hope for Survivors. Its message is clear—that in the midst of hard times, one can still find tranquility. Sometimes a Survivor may feel guilty about finding moments of calm while their life has been turned upside down. However, everyone deserves a break from sadness, sorrow, and troubles. In fact, those breaks renew our strength so we can better navigate the tough times. So, cherish any glimpses of happiness you find and know that the future holds the possibility of more good days.

**Survivor Strategies**:

Think: What would peace feel like for you? What peace have you had in your "valley"? How did you feel before, during and after that period? How do you feel now?

Do: Find one positive thing that will make you smile and/or bring you peace; then do it.

**Supporter Strategies**:

Think: Have you seen the Survivor experience peace? What has brought on that peace?

Do: Help the Survivor to create a list of peaceful activities, then refer to and use it as appropriate.

**Your Reflections**:

What's on your mind and in your heart after reading this entry and pondering the questions? In light of this, what will you do?

# CHAPTER 18

# ENCOUNTERING THE NEW NORMAL

*January 1, 2010, written seven months after Ralph's death*

D EAR Ralph,

We are now into a new year, and it's the first time in twenty-four years when you have not been either a step or a phone call away. This is different. It is the "new normal." I can't help but think about what I've lost and what I'm missing. I want you here beside me to go through life's ups and downs, to make the hard decisions, and to laugh at the silly things and inside jokes that only you and I understand. I want to cuddle with you at night, to ask you if I should let one of the boys go to a friend's house, and to tell you all about my crazy day and my endless dreams.

With your death, I have lost a friend for today and all the fantasies I had for tomorrow. With time, the thought of your peace will grow more and more comforting to me, while the thought of all I have lost in this world will become less and less painful. That, my love, is the healing that will eventually come as I make my way through the grief process.

Now that I've got that out, I have decided that in 2010, I will stop feeling sorry for myself and will instead feel good about all we shared and created. As I move forward into a new season of life, I will concentrate on being a good mom to our children, a good daughter, a good sister, a good friend, a good person, and a good example of God's love and grace. I was originally tempted to use the word "great." However, I think it's important to worry less about being perfect and more about just "being."

I know I will stumble and fall, and I will have setbacks, tears and moments of doubt. But that is but a small portion of what is to come. As I learned in church earlier today, I will also have joy, peace, happiness, and comfort, along with celebrations and accomplishments that may exceed my wildest dreams. At the end of this new decade, our children should all be college graduates and my life should be a testament to resilience, mercy, and faith. Right after midnight, my grandmother called me to tell me that she knows you're rejoicing in heaven as you hold Isaiah in your arms. She also said that you will be with me always. Well, my love, keep holding our beautiful baby, keep laughing that wonderful laugh, and smiling that beautiful smile. Keep looking down on us and know that I will build upon the foundation we created together, and more importantly, I will keep God at the center of my heart, mind, and decisions. It's time to rest now, so I'll say goodnight. I love you!

**My Reflections**:

> I don't remember making this pledge. Perhaps that's why I've done more stumbling than standing this year. Perhaps that's the beauty of keeping a journal; it reminds us of our aspirations and helps us to make corrections as needed. What I do remember about this entry is how life adjusts for a Survivor and the idea of what is "normal" changes. Normal is what we become accustomed to, and death tends to shatter our sense of normalcy, often being an unwanted intrusion into a world we think we've made sense of. So, it's easy to see the difficulties related to the death of someone who plays an integral role in our daily lives, as well as in the future that we've imagined for ourselves. Hence, normal isn't so normal anymore, and both Survivors and Supporters have to adjust their perception in order to find a "new normal."

That's tough when our hearts and minds are so firmly rooted in the past and our loss. So acceptance of a "new normal" will take a conscious effort to adjust to a new life and all the changes that come with it. This may involve new roles, new partnerships, new confidence, new friendships, and much more. That's a lot to deal with! Yet, this is also a time filled with opportunities to focus less on what you've lost and more on what you still have, less on who you were and more on the good parts of who you are now, and less on your weakness and more on the strength that's deep within you. The simple gesture of focusing on the light may be an incredible way to bring you out of the darkness. In doing so, you will build a "new normal" piece by piece until that small light grows, and together with the memory of your loved one, floods you with a new peace.

**Survivor Strategies**:

Think: Describe what normal was like before your loss. How has your life changed? What is most important to as you move toward your "new normal"?

Do: Imagine where (and who) you want to be one year from now. Write down those thoughts, then decide and record what needs to happen for you to get there.

**Supporter Strategies**:

Think: Describe what normal was like before the loss. How has life changed for you and the Survivor? What is most important as both of you move toward your "new normal"?

Do: Imagine where (and who) you want to be one year from now. Write down those thoughts, then decide and record what

needs to happen for you to get there. Initiate a discussion with
the Survivor regarding each of your responses, so that you both
have an opportunity to share and help one another.

**Your Reflections**:

What's on your mind and in your heart after reading this entry
and pondering the questions? In light of this, what will you do?

# Chapter 19

# Reliving the Loss

*January 2, 2010, written fifteen years after Mom's death*

D EAR Mom,

One of your former co-workers told me a funny story about you today! She then talked about how she still can't believe you're gone. For some reason, that made me think about the last day of your life. The saddest part is I just didn't know how good I had it. I had my dream job and two wonderful little boys. The only thing that would have made my life better would have been if my marriage was on the right course, which it wasn't at that time. But, hey, everything can't always be perfect!

After a few days of me teaching a class with you as a participant (I loved that look of pride in your eyes), I got to be your escort for a company anniversary party that night. I think you were being honored for twenty-five years of service. Before the party, I remember you sitting in my kitchen waiting for me. Was that sadness I detected in you? It reminded me of a few days earlier when, in your hotel room, I was sharing my marital woes. I told you that sometimes it was hard for me to understand what my husband was feeling, because his mom had died and mine was still alive. To this day, I remember you just staring at me (with that same face you had in my kitchen) and not commenting (which was odd for you). But, I was young and I just shook it off.

Do you remember us leaving my house in a great mood and having an absolutely wonderful time at the party? It's all still so clear to me.

On our way back to Frederick, we had a pretty deep conversation about death. You told me that a friend of yours had just gone to a funeral of someone who had been driving along, minding her business, when a car came across the center line and took that person's life. You reminded me that life could end in an instant; you then told me where your will was if anything ever happened to you. When we got back to Frederick, I dropped you off at your car and waved goodbye. You then drove home with Tia.

A few hours later, my phone rang and I awoke from a deep sleep. Who would be calling at this time of night? At first, it was Tia on the phone, and she said she was at the hospital. Aunt Flora must have grabbed the phone from her, because next I heard her yelling, "Get to the hospital, there's been an accident." At that moment, I knew the outcome would not be good. I woke up Ralph, and he got William ready. Tre was with his grandparents. As I paced back and forth chanting, "No God, no God, please no," Ralph hustled me to the car. When we finally arrived at the emergency room, we were guided into a special room. Boy, do I hate those rooms; little did I know that I'd visit them many more times in the future.

As soon as we walked through the door, I saw Tia sitting beside Aunt Flora who then blurted out, "Denise, she's gone." At that moment something left my body, and I had no energy, strength, or direction. I immediately collapsed. Once they got me together, I was told that you had been driving home with Tia when a drunk driver came across the center line and hit you straight on. Tia watched you take your last breath. The only thing I could think was, "What will I do without my best friend?" The doctor then came in and explained that you had died almost instantly from trauma. She then asked if we wanted to see you. We went into the room and there you were on a table, my beautiful mother looking as if you were asleep. Why did this have to happen?

The days that followed were a blur: calling friends (grueling), making funeral arrangements (draining), handling business (confusing), and adjusting to living without you, my "life force" (depressing). We never did find your will, because I had blocked out what you told me in the car that night. In the weeks that followed, I moved out of my home, left Ralph, and showed him I was through by getting a legal separation. I recklessly drowned my pain in another relationship that I thought was fun and was helping me escape my new reality. I also began experiencing headaches that are with me to this day. In fact, for a period back then, I was hospitalized because the pain was so bad. I now believe that my body was trying to force me to deal with this tragedy (something I was trying hard to avoid).

In the three years after your death, I went through a re-birth of sorts. First, I saw a therapist for the first time in my life. That was a lifesaver! Second, I read books on grief, and specifically, on losing your mother. Third, based on what I'm sure was your voice prompting us, Tia and I decided to stop being victims and to wage a campaign (including a rally, newspaper articles, a petition, and more) to ensure that your killer would receive jail time. While he was only sentenced to eighteen months of jail time, I believe it was more than he would have received had we been silent. Finally, after a one-year separation from Ralph, we reunited, and soon after, I became pregnant with what would be your third grandson.

While I was nervous about the fact that this would be the first time that I'd give birth to a child and you wouldn't be there, the night I went into labor with him, I awoke to your all-time favorite movie on TV. I also gave birth to him on the same day you gave birth to Tia. I guess that was your way of being with me once again. You continue to be with me in the little ways that I act and think like you, in Tia's recollections and funny stories, and in the memories that will forever be in my heart!

Mom, I know you're looking down on me and saying you're glad I finally got some sense. I can almost hear your voice. You were right when you told me (following your mom's death) that you never get over the loss of your mother. While my wound from your death has healed, the scar will always be there. And, that's okay! I have come to accept the moments (like Mother's Day) when I feel sorry for myself, because I don't have you here with me. I simply acknowledge the pain and then go on to reflect on all that I was (and still am) blessed with. In the same way, on days like today when I feel like reliving your last day, I accept the heartache of the moment, and then I embrace all that I had in those thirty years you were here with me on earth, and all that I have now because you gave birth to me, loved me, and provided a strong and lasting foundation for my future. Thank you, Mommy!

**My Reflections**:

It feels really good to tell the story of my mother's last day. That may sound morbid, but I want to make sure that this story can be shared with my children. When someone you love dies, it's as if you're caught in the middle of a whirlwind. You're in shock and things feel as if they're moving in slow motion. Yet, when you look back on that time, things may have felt as if they moved so fast that you could hardly catch your breath and keep up. And so, without reflection, it's hard to understand and process what really happened. As such, it can be extremely helpful to periodically revisit the loss. What happened beforehand? How did you find out? What did you do afterward? How did you feel? How did others around you react and support you? When did the healing begin? How did that happen?

That analysis, whether it's done alone, with a friend, or with a trained professional, can play an important role in your healing process. In addition, there is power in the written word. Putting your story on paper allows you to "get it all out" and examine various aspects of what happened, how you were feeling, and how others interacted with you. It also allows you to reflect on what you learned, what you would have done differently, what you needed in that situation, and more. Then, when you desire to do so in the future, you can share your story with others and/or revisit and reprocess that information in a healthy and productive way. Doing so can also help you to let go of the person's death while moving to a place where you spend more time celebrating the person's life. When you get to that point, putting as much or more energy into sharing or recording memories of the person's life can be even more rewarding.

**Survivor Strategies**:

Think: Have you ever taken the time to record what happened before and after your loss? If so, how did that help you, and if not, how could that help you now and in the future?

Do: As a way to release some of the pain of your loss, write a summary of everything that happened, including your emotions, what led up to it, and what happened afterward. Then, record your best memories of the person's life.

**Supporter Strategies**:

Think: How might it help the Survivor to reflect on (and record) details of the loss? What's a good way to document the survivor's best memories?

Do: Find people and resources that can help the Survivor process memories.

**Your Reflections**:

What's on your mind and in your heart after reading this entry and pondering the questions? In light of this, what will you do?

# CHAPTER 20

# DEALING WITH PHYSICAL PAIN

*January 3, 2010, written seven months after Ralph's death*

D EAR Ralph,

Tonight, once again, I'm not feeling well. Sometimes I wonder if my body is reacting to the grief and showing me that there are still issues I need to deal with. I feel that there are too many days when I'm in pain. Sometimes it's a headache; other times it is shoulder and neck pain. Recently, I had to go to the emergency room because my neck and back pain was so bad. Today, Malcolm told me that he really wants me to take care of my health, because he doesn't want the same thing that happened to his dad to happen to me. That made me even sadder, because I am painfully aware of how our children worry about losing their remaining parent.

In the days and weeks to come, I'm going to have to be a lot more proactive about my health. That includes visiting doctors as needed, having a healthier diet, and exercising more. I pray for the help and strength to do this for our sons. In addition, I pray to be able to do this for myself, because I can't keep feeling like this. In fact, I need to say goodnight to you now because of the pain shooting through my neck. I wish you were here to tell me all will be okay. But you're not, and I can't change that. I just hope that one day this loneliness, longing, and pain will leave me. Goodnight.

**My Reflections**:

> Reading this reminds me that the power and capability of the human mind is incredible. Think about how our brains control our activities, allow us to process information and draw conclusions, and are the command station for most complex machine ever: the human body. So, it's not unreasonable to think that when we are not dealing with a painful issue in our conscious mind, our subconscious mind can send out signals that indicate we're in trouble. Those signals might include weight loss, weight gain, headaches, shooting pains, or other symptoms. For a Survivor, the interpretation of those signals and symptoms may sometimes be traced to a couple sources. First is the notion that our unresolved mental pain is being manifested in a physical way. Another source could be that one's health is neglected during the process of grieving, which in turn, leads to physical health issues. In either case, it is important during the grief process to pay close attention to both physical and mental health. Doing so is a key component of both short-term and long-term healing.

**Survivor Strategies**:

> Think: How are you feeling, both physically and mentally? If you realize there's a need for assistance, who can you turn to for help?

> Do: Keep a journal of how you are feeling both physically and mentally. Seek help from professionals if there are ongoing issues.

**Supporter Strategies**:

Think: How does the Survivor appear to be doing, both physically and mentally? Are there any resources she would benefit from? How is your physical and mental health? What assistance or resources do you need?

Do: Ask the Survivor when she had her last physical and encourage her to schedule one if it's overdue and/or if there are recurring health issues.

**Your Reflections**:

What's on your mind and in your heart after reading this entry and pondering the questions? In light of this, what will you do?

# CHAPTER 21

# BEING A SECONDARY
# SURVIVOR

*January 6, 2010, written three years after Aunt Flora's death*

D EAR Aunt Flora,

Today, on the anniversary of your death, I'm thinking about a day in December three years ago when I told my therapist that it had been over a year since Isaiah died and I was ready to take my "mourning cloak" off. I just felt like it was time to smile again and to move forward with life. However, less than a month later I was propelled into yet another tragedy. I remember walking outside after my sons' basketball games, looking up into the January sky, and allowing the sun to caress my face. I actually felt good. What pulled me back into reality was the ringing of Tia's cell phone. Her expression immediately turned somber and she told me to let my cousin, Joy, take the kids to my dad's house. Not long after, a police officer informed me that you were hit and killed instantly in a car accident. I recall being unable to control my shaking body as we rushed down to the hospital and yet another private room. It was uncanny that losing you hit me almost as hard as Mom's death. The similarity was unbelievable; she was killed by a drunk driver and your life was taken by a drag racer. The two of you died only miles apart. One difference was that with Mom's death I was in charge since I was one of her children. While you treated me like a daughter, in truth I wasn't your child, so I had little say in some of the decisions that were made after you died. More than that, one doesn't usually get the same kind of sympathy when an aunt dies (as opposed to a mother). Perhaps that's why I felt like I mourned you in silence.

Aunt Flora, I was not your child by birth and the world would not recognize me as yours, nor would I ask people to do so. But, I would like to recognize you as someone who treated me as if I were your daughter. You were proud of my accomplishments, interested in my activities, and involved with my family and my life. Thank you for filling part of the void left by Mom. Thanks also for being a key connection to Mom's side of the family, something Tia and I desperately needed, especially in the early days after her death. As my therapist helped me to realize, it was natural for me to grieve the loss of your love and support, even if the world didn't recognize that grief. While it still hurts when I think about how you too were taken from me, I am thankful for the time we had together and the role we played in each other's lives. Thank you, my aunt, friend, and surrogate mom!

**My Reflections**:

> This entry makes me smile as I remember my "crazy Aunt Flo." I also feel sad as I think about the loneliness I felt as I mourned her death. It is natural during a loss for all of the attention to go to the deceased person's significant other, children, and parents. But with any death, there are also "Secondary Survivors." These are the people who may not have the title, blood, and/ or legal relationship, but they grieve deeply nonetheless. These are folks who had a tight emotional bond with the decedent and will mourn the loss of their relationship and the role the person played in their lives. This type of pain can be just as strong as the grief that results from more recognized bonds. The problem occurs when this grief is unacknowledged, unrecognized, or dismissed, causing further pain for the Survivor who is in this position. Being sensitive to all types of loss and all types

of Survivors allows us as a community "to grieve together" and help each other adapt to the loss.

**Survivor Strategies:**

Think: Do you have any unrecognized losses? Is there anyone associated with your current loss who might feel like a "Secondary Survivor"? If so, would it be worthwhile to reach out to that person?

Do: Do something to acknowledge your own "secondary loss" or reach out to someone else who's experienced such a loss.

**Supporter Strategies:**

Think: As a Supporter, has your own loss been secondary to that of the Survivor? What assistance do you need with your own grief process?

Do: Find a grief support group that will allow you to deal with your loss.

**Your Reflections:**

What's on your mind and in your heart after reading this entry and pondering the questions? In light of this, what will you do?

# CHAPTER 22

# RECONCILING SYMBOLS OF THE PAST

*January 7, 2010, written seven months after Ralph's death*

DEAR Ralph,

I wanted to tell you about a conversation I had at dinner with the boys. I'm not sure why it came up, but we were talking about me wearing my wedding rings. I told them that I had to get used to not wearing them anymore. Malcolm then wanted to know why I wouldn't wear them. When I told him that it was because I wasn't married anymore, he said that I was still married and that it was more of a spiritual marriage. Wow! How do you respond to that? Is he right?

A friend of mine was over last weekend and she commented that she viewed me as still being married (which meant I should still have my rings on). So, should I be wearing the rings or not? When I wear them around people who know me and know you have died, I feel like they probably feel sorry for me and wonder why I can't let go. When I don't wear them around people who don't know us, I feel bad, because I think they probably look at us with pity thinking I've never been married.

Okay, as I write this, I can already hear your words in response: *why is this all about what other people think? What do you think? What do you want to do?* The answer is that I just don't know. I am still committed to you. I know that I am still married to you. You're just not here physically.

However, if I'm honest, I cannot stand the prospect of being alone for the rest of my life. You know that I would give anything to have you here with me. But, if I can't have you, I do want some type of companionship—especially when the boys leave home in a few years. So, with that in mind, I guess I have no clear answers. I think I'll just continue to wear my ring (or one of the special rings I purchased after you died) whenever I choose.

I know I need to worry less about other people and more about what's in my heart. You tried to teach me that when you were here beside me. Please know that I haven't forgotten the wise words you shared. They're still in my heart, and I won't forget them, nor will I forget you. No matter what decisions I make in the future and whether or not I have my wedding rings on, you will always be a part of me, and I will always look forward to reuniting with you in the next life. I'll try to make sure all of this isn't confusing for the boys; they're the only ones I should be worried about. Most of all, I'll pray and meditate on my actions as I move forward. That's the guidance (and relationship) I need most. Goodnight, my dear.

**My Reflections:**

> I still wonder how we move forward when there are constant reminders of the past. If the past is always with us, how do we carry on without being stuck? How do we ever stop revisiting the same issues? These questions can be perplexing for a Survivor. Moreover, the answers aren't necessarily easy, and they're not the same for everyone. Each individual must decide the right timing for various decisions. For a spouse, it may be when or if to stop wearing a wedding band. For a parent of a deceased child, it may be whether or when to do something with the child's clothes or bedroom. Each relationship and situation is unique.
>
> Support groups or individual therapy can be extremely helpful

in dealing with the many questions that arise during grief. Such resources allow Survivors and Supporters to put the questions in context and gain a better sense of what others experience and how they've adapted. While some have thought of therapy as something a weak person would seek out, it actually requires an act of strength to reach out for help and perspective. In the process, one can learn effective strategies for moving forward while honoring the past.

**Survivor Strategies**:

Think: What symbols of the past are you dealing with? How do those symbols make you feel? Is the presence of those symbols hurting or helping you?

Do: Research the grief support groups and therapists in your area; then consider how they may be able to assist you.

**Supporter Strategies**:

Think: How are symbols of the past impacting you? How do you see them impacting the Survivor? What else is hurting you and/or the Survivor?

Do: Research the grief support groups and therapists in your area; then consider how they may be able to assist the Survivor and/or you.

**Your Reflections**:

What's on your mind and in your heart after reading this entry and pondering the questions? In light of this, what will you do?

# CHAPTER 23

# DECIDING WHEN IT'S
# TIME TO MOVE ON

*January 27, 2010, written seven months after Ralph's death*

**D**EAR Ralph,

Men are funny! Within the last week, I've had two close male friends ask me about whether I was dating. Do they not understand that it hasn't even been a year yet? They really mean well, but it's so interesting that men just move on. In talking to Joy about this, she reminded me that many men remarry within a year of their spouses dying. Honey, I remember you used to say that if I died you'd mourn for the appropriate time and then move on. The implication was that the length of time wouldn't be too long. You meant it to be funny, but there was an element of truth to it. The key is that "the appropriate time" is based on the individual person.

Right now dear, I'm still your wife. I know I need to move forward at some point, especially because of the loneliness I feel right now. However, for now, I choose to mourn you and heal at my own pace. My choices only have to be okay with me. Wow, it sounds like I'm finally developing some confidence (and that feels good). Good night, my dear husband. I love you!

**My Reflections**:

This entry is funny and insightful. I actually learned in one of my graduate school classes that men do tend to remarry much faster than women do for a variety of reasons. I believe that moving on can be a sensitive matter. If a Survivor takes too long, they may be pitied as someone who's stuck in time and can't move forward. If a Survivor moves on too quickly, it may be assumed that he or she didn't really love the person who died. And so, this delicate dance ensues.

Ultimately, society can't judge nor determine the perfect time for anyone to move forward. Instead, the Survivor is the one who needs to make that decision. In doing so, the Survivor can benefit from being open to the thoughts and feelings of others, while also being comfortable following his or her own instincts and heart. One reason for being sensitive to the insights of others is because the Survivor's judgment may be slightly skewed because of the emotional rollercoaster associated with grief. And so, outside input that is sought after may be greatly appreciated. In the end, being confident in our own choices can be the greatest reward of all.

**Survivor Strategies**:

Think: What does "moving forward" mean to you? When will you know it's the right time to move on? Whose input will help you decide? When you do move on, who will be impacted? Is there anything you should do to aid in the transition of those impacted by your decision?

Do: Identify one area where you may need to move forward and create an action plan for doing so.

**Supporter Strategies**:

Think: What advice have you given the Survivor about moving forward? What advice should you give the Survivor about moving on? How can you do so in a way that's appreciated and not resented?

Do: Be ready to talk if the Survivor brings up the topic of moving on.

**Your Reflections**:

What's on your mind and in your heart after reading this entry and pondering the questions? In light of this, what will you do?

# CHAPTER 24

# ACKNOWLEDGING THE PAIN OF OTHERS

*January 29, 2010, written fifteen years after Mom's death*

DEAR Mom,

Yesterday, Tia was talking about this year marking the fifteenth anniversary of your death. As she was talking, I sensed deep sadness within her. She then called this morning in tears. All these months, she's been working so hard to support me as I grieve Ralph's passing. In doing that, it was easy for me to forget that she carries her own pain as well. She also lost Ralph, who was like a brother to her, Isaiah, who was more than just a nephew to her, and Aunt Flora, who was more like her than she'd ever admit. Added to that is the pain of losing you, her mom, something I think she's never truly resolved.

As I think about my sister, I realize that while we both lost a mother, we grieve differently. I grieve the loss of you as my best friend and confidante. She grieves the fact that your relationship wasn't all she wanted it to be. Even deeper, she deals with the pain of watching you die and the guilt of wishing she had been driving that night so your life would have been spared. Fifteen years later, she still can't drive on the road where you died.

I hurt because Tia's hurting, yet I'm not sure how to help her. That's an odd thing for me to admit as I've spent so much time studying grief, yet can't help one of the key people who's supported me. That just goes to show that no one knows everything, especially when it comes to grief. As for today, I dropped what I was doing this morning and spent time with her. We also went to your gravesite, something that means a lot to Tia. So, I'm sure you're pretty happy that your girls are not at each other's throats and instead are together as a loving family. You built that foundation, and I thank you for that!

By the end of the day, Tia was laughing again (and so was I). As we move forward, I am going to try to spend a little less time focused on my own pain and a little more energy reaching out to her. I will encourage Tia to address her own grief journey. Mom, you always said, "When you don't have anyone else, you have family." I promise to remember that as my sister and I become two people who can help one another to grieve together! I love you, Mom!

**My Reflections**:

>Since this entry, my sister, Tia, made the choice to drive on the road where our mother died. On the day that happened, she called me full of tears and full of pride that she had made it over that hurdle. Celebrating this milestone with her and helping her through her episode on the day of this journal entry actually helped to take my mind off my own pain. When we are hurting, it's all about us. In fact, the grieving process is one time when we can truly justify being self-centered. After all, we must begin our own healing before we can be a help to others.

>There are, however, moments when it's good to take a time-out to be sensitive to the needs of those around us. In doing so, there will be circumstances when we're not equipped to help others due to the timing, relationship, skills needed, or other factors. These can be handled with a simple gesture such as telling the person that you know she's in pain and that while you are not in a position to personally help at the time, you would suggest

that they reach out to another friend or counselor. If you're in a different place and able to assist, helping someone else through her trial can be a welcome respite and a great way to give back to others.

**Survivor Strategies**:

Think: Who else do you know who's grieving? Are there any ways you can help that person? If you're not in a position to help, how else can you be sensitive to the needs of other Survivors or Supporters?

Do: Reach out to a Survivor or Supporter with a simple note, conversation, or other meaningful gesture.

**Supporter Strategies**:

Think: As a Supporter, are you suppressing your own grief in an effort to help the Survivor? If so, who can you turn to in order to get the help and support you need?

Do: Reach out to someone and share your own grief.

**Your Reflections**:

What's on your mind and in your heart after reading this entry and pondering the questions? In light of this, what will you do?

# CHAPTER 25

# DANCING AGAIN

*January 30, 2010, written seven months after Ralph's death*

D<sup>EAR</sup> Ralph,

Guess what? I just realized that for the past two weeks, I've been getting up, putting on my music, then singing and dancing in the mornings. I've found myself actually feeling pretty good afterwards! Why is that significant? It's because on those occasions I'm not waking up with sadness as my constant companion. More than that, when I realized what I was doing I wasn't overwhelmed with feelings of guilt about having moments of happiness. I hate it when other people say I'm moving on (although I use that term myself), because it sounds as if I've left you behind. Instead, I think it's that I'm healing. That means you're still here with me. I think you'd be proud of me, and that makes me feel good.

Ralph, some part of me will always be grieving your death. At the same time, I know I'm not supposed to be in a constant state of sadness. The boys need more than that from me. I also know I need more than that! Thank you for all you gave me while you were here beside me, along with the ways you changed me and became a part of me. I know I'll still have my sad moments, yet I'm encouraged that I'm at a place where it's okay to heal. I take a lot of comfort in that! I love you, honey!

**My Reflections**:

That entry was definitely written in a moment of peace. When there have been so many bad days, it's hard to believe that a good day is possible. More than that, happiness can be a foreign feeling that seems wrong when you've been stuck in a place where you believe that things are never going to get better. Some of us have heard the platitudes about time healing all wounds and politely smiled as we thought to ourselves that the person just didn't have a clue about grief.

What we knew for sure was that we would never heal and we would never get over our loss. So, if we're feeling good, it might seem like a betrayal of our loved one. How dare we? Well, with time comes an ability to see that life has good days (or moments) and bad, ups and downs. While our lives will never be the same as they were before our loved ones died, we are still alive. This means that the sun will continue to shine on our faces, even on those days when we don't feel great inside. It also means that it may rain on those days when we feel sunshine from within. That's okay because life is complex and so are we. So, on those days when we can sing and dance, let us rejoice in the moment, knowing that our loved one is probably dancing with us.

**Survivor Strategies**:

Think: When was the last time you did something enjoyable? How do you feel when you do something you enjoy?

Do: Get up and dance (or do something you find uplifting)!

**Supporter Strategies**:

Think: What do you think about singing, dancing, sunshine, and rain when it comes to both you and the Survivor? What do you both need more of? How can you get it?

Do: Go outside, take a nice walk, and enjoy the sunshine on your face; then encourage the Survivor to do something peaceful or enjoyable.

**Your Reflections**:

What's on your mind and in your heart after reading this entry and pondering the questions? In light of this, what will you do?

# CHAPTER 26

# FEELING GUILTY

*January 31, 2010, written seven months after Ralph's death*

**D**EAR Ralph,

Today I had a flashback to the last time you were home. I was sitting on the couch in the family room, and you came to sit down beside me. I'm not sure why, but it irritated me, and I went upstairs to bed. When I awoke the next morning, you had written me a note that said you had gone to the hospital and didn't want to wake me. You were considerate despite my rudeness. Then, I remembered our conversation at the hospital when you told me that I often didn't give you my full attention. I was irritated but knew you were right. The next morning when you really started to feel badly, you called and insisted that I come to the hospital to be with you. You still wanted me there despite my obvious faults. Ralph, I feel so guilty, because I could and should have been a better wife and human being. Why didn't I know to be more caring? Why didn't I realize that our time together would be so limited? Why did I put other people and things before you? Why didn't I pay more attention when you were sick at home and when you were hospitalized? Will you ever forgive me for my lack of sensitivity and attention? More than that, will I ever forgive myself? You and our relationship deserved so much more!

Ralph, I can't go back to change what's in the past; but I can change what happens in the future. You see, some of those same behaviors I exhibited with you are still part of the behaviors I show to those closest to me. That includes our children, my dad and sister. I am such a moody person. But, like with you, I never know the last time I'll talk to any one of them. As such, with today's reflection and realization, I pledge that I will actively work to change my behavior with family and friends. I will give them my full attention and not get irritated at little things. I will also do my best to cherish every single moment I have with them. That, my dear, will be my tribute to you. I hope that you're pleased by that. I love you, Ralph!

**My Reflections**:

> Boy was I plagued by a number of regrets! If only … I wish … Why didn't I … Why did I … The list can go on and on. Regrets when someone has died can be overwhelming. Sometimes, it's guilt over something we shouldn't have said or something we've done to hurt our loved one. Perhaps it's more time we should have spent or more attention we should have paid so that special person knew how much he meant to us. Other times, it's even more serious than that, and we think our actions could have resulted in our loved one living longer and not dying.

> Such guilt and regret can have long-range effects. It could cause prolonged or unresolved issues, mental anguish, and/or physical pain. Unfortunately, we can't go back in time to change what's already happened. So, we must find ways to forgive ourselves for whatever we did or didn't do, and then resolve to move forward while committing to behaviors that will not cause regret in the future. In doing so, it's important to remember that we'll never be perfect. So, we can live the best lives possible while being gentle with ourselves if we make missteps. Dealing with these missteps in a healthy way can lead to a healthy life and healthy relationships.

**Survivor Strategies**:

Think: Is there anything you feel guilty about? What is it and why? Because you can't go back in time, what can you commit to doing differently today and in the future?

Do: Make a list of everything you feel guilty about; select the issues that you're willing and able to deal with and then address them. Share this exercise with a Supporter.

**Supporter Strategies**:

Think: How is guilt impacting you? How have you seen guilt impact the Survivor? In what ways can the two of you help one another to resolve your issues with guilt?

Do: Make a list of everything you feel guilty about; select the issues that you're willing and able to deal with and then address them. Share this exercise with the Survivor.

**Your Reflections**:

What's on your mind and in your heart after reading this entry and pondering the questions? In light of this, what will you do?

# CHAPTER 27

# ENDURING MULTIPLE MILESTONES

*March 26, 2010, written nine months after Ralph's death*

D EAR Ralph,

Today is our first born's 18th birthday. After we did a morning celebration by singing to him and giving him his gifts (you know how he loves gift cards), I went into my bathroom to get ready for work. In the shower, my tears began and wouldn't stop. I never expected to celebrate this milestone with him and not have you here. I then thought about the other milestones that will occur this year. In a little over a week, you would have turned fifty. Right after that, Isaiah would have been five years old. Later this year, I'll be forty-five, Malcolm will become a teenager, and William will turn sixteen (and you know he can't wait to drive). Why do we have to experience all of these special moments without you being physically here with us? This morning, I cried more than I have in a long time. Maybe it was a good thing, though, because afterwards I felt cleansed and was okay to go about my day.

I know I will face many more sensitive days in the year to come, including the anniversary of Isaiah's death, Tre's graduation from high school, the anniversary of you dying, and so much more. I pray that God will give me the gift of remembering good times, along with the comfort of holding in my heart the best of you and the best of what we had. At the same time, I pray that whatever the kids are going through, they're able to share it with me, with someone else, with God, or process it themselves so that they may grow stronger with each passing day. Perhaps one day they will help others who are hurting also.

Finally, Ralph, I hope you're looking down on Tre and feeling the same pride I feel. I'm so grateful that you poured so much into him and that he had both of us for so long. All of our young men possess the values and love that you affectionately placed in them. Please keep helping me as I try to fulfill both our roles in their lives. I pray that I will remember your wisdom and strength, combine it with my gentleness and passion, and be the parent our children deserve. As always, thanks for listening to me and thanks for loving us. We miss and love you!

**My Reflections**:

> I'm not sure why the intensity of my emotions surprised me so much that day, but it did. I do recall that it was a tremendous release that prepared me for some of the other milestones I'd face. Some of the firsts that a Survivor will experience are obvious. This includes markers such as the first week, month, holiday, birthday, and anniversary without your loved one. Supporters may be more likely to notice these milestones and help Survivors through them. However, because life goes on, there is a chance that people may not remember. In addition, it is impossible for them to know about all of the other firsts you may experience. Examples include the first time you hear your favorite song, the first time you go on vacation without your loved one, the first time you come across something in the deceased person's handwriting or with their scent, and more. The list is endless, and there's no way to prepare or arrange for someone to be there to support you through every experience you'll be confronted with.

> In dealing with these reminders, sometimes your response will

include sadness and tears. That's okay. Other times, you may laugh or smile. Even still, you might not even realize the milestone until it's all over. Whatever the response, don't be too hard on yourself. In addition, don't hesitate to identify strategies, people, and other resources to help you, especially because you may experience various firsts for the rest of your life.

**Survivor Strategies**:

Think: What firsts have you dealt with already? How did you deal with them? What are the firsts that you're most nervous about dealing with?

Do: Think about the firsts you have coming up and how/if you'd like to acknowledge them.

**Supporter Strategies**:

Think: What firsts are coming up for the Survivor? How do you think the Survivor would want you to acknowledge those firsts?

Do: Create a list of upcoming "firsts," and then ask the Survivor if there's anything he/she would like to do to acknowledge or handle that "first."

**Your Reflections**:

What's on your mind and in your heart after reading this entry and pondering the questions? In light of this, what will you do?

# CHAPTER 28

# LAUGHING AGAIN

*April 3, 2010, written ten months after Ralph's death*

D EAR Ralph,

This morning, the boys came into my room one by one. Eventually, it was the four of us lying on my bed. I smiled as they joked with me and one another. There was a lot of laughter and silliness. It reminded me of old times and made me grateful for the healing that's taking place for each of them. The resiliency of our boys is truly amazing and encouraging! Naturally, I started singing our "We're Together" song that we always sang when the whole family was in the same room. Believe it or not, the boys all joined in. As they left the room to go play video games together, I felt really happy that they have one another!

Tomorrow would have been your fiftieth birthday. And so, your sisters are coming up today. Our families will then go to the cemetery and release fifty balloons to commemorate that special day. That was Malcolm's idea, and I think it's really special! Tomorrow, forty members of my dad's side of the family are coming over for Easter dinner. I decided to invite everyone so that I'm not sitting here feeling depressed all day. I want your birthday to be a happy day. Your friend, Doc, is stopping by in the morning after he places flowers on your grave. I hope that thought makes you smile! Next week, we leave for Hawaii on Isaiah's birthday. The boys are excited that we'll all be vacationing together!

Ralph, as I reflect on the morning and think about tomorrow and the week to come, I am grateful for the fact that the boys and I are able to laugh and sing together and not be constantly overwhelmed with sadness when thinking about the fact that you and Isaiah are not here with us. These are the moments that give me hope. Yes, our lives have had some very hard moments. Dealing with the deaths of people you love deeply is always hard. So, the pain is still there. But as I think about all we've made it through and all we continue to deal with, I still have hope, joy, and peace. We all imagine a life without hurt and pain. But that's just not realistic.

What's realistic is knowing there will be difficult moments and understanding we all can make it through. I hurt so much because I loved you so much. But, like today, eventually there are fewer moments of pain and more moments of joy and peace that come with healing and holding you close to my heart.

Ralph, we're going to be okay. We will never be the same, but we will be alright. Darling, as you continue to watch over us as we go through life, know that you are (and always will be) a part of every single one of us. Thank you for what you poured into us, for the relationships you built with each of us, and for the unconditional love you gave. We are still together, just in a different way. Finally, I want you to know that while I may not write letters to you forever, we will continue to communicate constantly in my thoughts and heart. And, I have a sneaking suspicion that the same thing is happening with our boys! We love and thank you!

**My Reflections**:

> Oops! I laughed. How horrible! Wow, I smiled. How unbeliev-able! Sounds silly, doesn't it? But, these may be the thoughts that could torment a Survivor who doesn't know that it's okay to have a good day. In fact, with healing comes more and more good days. Those good days do not minimize the impact of the person who died, nor does it mean we didn't love that person.

What it means is that life moves forward and that it's okay for us to move forward with it.

Think about what happens if we get a cut on our arm. In treating the wound, we will have to clean it out, which will help us in the long run but could hurt in the short run. We then find that a scab develops and there may still be some discomfort or pain as the scab assists with our healing. Eventually, the wound heals totally. There is often a scar left, but it doesn't hurt like it did in the beginning. Losing a loved one can be like a wound that will eventually heal but leaves a scar, representing the mark our loved one made on our lives. Just as it's okay to cry when we have a physical wound, it's also okay to cry with grief. The same applies with laughter, and in many cases, that laughter can be a great antiseptic for healing the wounds caused by grief.

**Survivor Strategies**:

Think: When was the last time you laughed? What made you laugh? Who can you share your laughter with?

Do: Find a positive activity that will make you laugh or smile; then find ways to indulge in that activity on a regular basis.

**Supporter Strategies**:

Think: When was the last time you laughed? When was the last time you laughed with the Survivor? How can you find ways to laugh or smile together more?

Do: Plan something positive and fun to do today on your own or with the Survivor.

**Your Reflections**:

What's on your mind and in your heart after reading this entry and pondering the questions? In light of this, what will you do?

# CHAPTER 29

# FORGETTING A SPECIAL DAY

*April 7, 2010, written five years after Isaiah's death*

DEAR Isaiah,

Today would have been your fifth birthday. What's a little crazy is that I actually forgot. Your brothers and I were supposed to leave for a business trip to Hawaii today. Because it's always hectic before leaving for a seven-day trip, I was going in a million different directions. Well, we ended up leaving late for the airport and arrived seven minutes after the cutoff for boarding the plane. I was in tears! Eventually, we were told that we'd have to leave at the same time tomorrow. When I called your Aunt Tia, she tried to console me by telling me that we could meet at the cemetery to release balloons in the afternoon, and we'd have lunch afterward.

When I hung up, I wondered out loud why she'd want to go to the cemetery today. That's when one of your brothers laughed at me and asked if I even knew it was my son's birthday. I could not believe that I forgot it was your birthday! Your brother then made it even worse by smiling and joking, "Some mother you are."

Sweetie, no one could have ever told me that I'd ever forget one of your birthdays. I am so sorry! I obviously had too much on my mind. I may have even been avoiding the thought because of this being the first year that we'd have to mark your birthday without your dad being there. I remember your birthday last year; we had been out of town at a funeral, and it was really late by the time we were free to go to the cemetery. Despite my protests, your dad insisted that we all go to your gravesite at about 9:00 PM. A cemetery is really dark and scary at night! But, your father insisted, and your brothers and I complied. It shows how much he loved you (or maybe how crazy your dad was).

In any case, I now have fond memories of us being there as a family last year, as well as of us being there as a family this year. We will be together as a family again, but until then we'll live our lives to the fullest as we cherish the memories of both you and your father. Happy fifth birthday, my angel. I hope you're having a heavenly celebration!

**My Reflections:**

> Reading this entry reminds me of how much I miss my son, yet how much I have progressed because I was able to make light of what occurred this year. When the pain of loss is fresh, it's unimaginable that you'd ever forget a special day like the birthday of your loved one. In fact, a Survivor may get mad at others for forgetting something so special. However, whether we like it or not, life goes on. First, it goes on for those people around you. Then, believe it or not, it goes on for the Survivor. When others forget, it does not mean that your loved one was not loved or that people are not sensitive to your needs. It just means they're human and that often they're juggling a lot more than the loss. In the same way, a Survivor forgetting a special occasion related to the deceased person is not an indictment on the Survivor or his/her love for the person who has died. Instead, it means that the Survivor is human, and is often juggling a lot more than the loss. Be gentle with yourself if this happens to you. If it bothers you too much, find ways to remind yourself in the future and then move forward with the knowledge that no gesture or oversight could ever define the love and respect you had (and still have) for the person who has died.

**Survivor Strategies**:

Think: How would you feel if you forgot a special date? What could you do to avoid that?

Do: Get a calendar and mark it with the special dates related to your loved one, as well as special dates related to the loved ones of others you care about.

**Supporter Strategies**:

Think: Have you ever forgotten a special date related to someone close's loss? How did you feel about it? What did you do about it? How can you avoid that in the future?

Do: Get a calendar and mark it with the special dates related to your own losses, as well as those of the people you care most about.

**Your Reflections**:

What's on your mind and in your heart after reading this entry and pondering the questions? In light of this, what will you do?

# CHAPTER 30

# APPRECIATING TODAY & ANTICIPATING TOMORROW

*June 10, 2010, written one year after Ralph's death*

# DEAR God,

This morning I wanted to reach out to you with my journal. I love you dearly, yet I'm still mad at you at times. Of course, what I'm mad about is all the death. Who wants to be separated from their loved ones? As I approach the one year anniversary of Ralph's death, I'm also sad that I'm still in so much pain. You'd think that this would get easier with time, but there are moments when I'm still overwhelmed. As such, I continue to need your help. I guess the good news is that I have far more moments when I am thankful for you speaking to me, especially through people. These Supporters have truly allowed me to heal and be a Survivor. Looking back five years to my "grateful" letter, I realize that I continue to be thankful today:

**For Family**:

> For Ralph, Isaiah, Mom and Aunt Flora being in my life, no matter how short the time was. I cherish those relationships, the love I received, and the lessons I learned from each one. Despite the pain, I wouldn't trade one moment with any of them!

For Ralph's sisters Sue and Lynn, and my Uncle Bobby and Aunt Joy miraculously being with me in the middle of the day on that fateful Friday when Ralph passed away. I couldn't even stand after Ralph's heart rate started to plummet, and we were rushed out of his room, so I can only imagine the added pain had I been there alone.

For my dad and stepmother for opening their home to us as soon as I came home from the hospital. They hosted my friends and put up a barrier of protection to make sure we'd be okay. Most of all, they just loved us and continued helping me raise these wonderful boys.

For Tia and Joy functioning as bookends, crutches, or whatever term describes the act of holding me up and not letting me fall. Tia just kept coming back despite my moods and weaknesses, while Joy kept reminding me to be gentle with myself and brought levity and substance during our weekly "fellowship" meetings.

For my beautiful sons who experienced their pain, shared it with me at times, and still had the strength to look after their mom. For all the days that I laid in my bed, couldn't move, and couldn't make them anything to eat, they didn't complain. They just tried to help me by helping themselves and one another.

For Uncle Bobby showing the meaning of acts of service as he helped us rent out our old home and then served as my own personal handyman. He didn't just help; he went above and beyond to make my walk easier, including heartwarming gestures such as making us his famous goulash!

For Aunt Karen, who always seemed to call me at the right moment.

For my grandmother who continued to offer a shoulder to lay my head on and for reminding me of how proud she is of how I've dealt with these hardships. Sometimes you need to hear that! Thank God our family has such a firm foundation!

**For Friendship**:

For friends like Cathy, Kim, and Chris who immediately flew or drove from far away to be by my side to help me through the funeral. It was also priceless to have Cathy make it a priority to come back in a few months (and make calls all along the way) just to make sure we were okay.

For my friend Dionne giving me the courage to ask for the time off I needed (two months) instead of what I thought was expected (two weeks) to get my life back together. She also helped with getting my benefits process rolling and later listened to me as I worried and cried about being able to get back to being the employee I once was. Between those practical things and our spiritual conversations, I see the gift her friendship and love were to me.

For countless co-workers who, led by my friend Missy, joined together and coordinated six months of continuous outreach to me and the boys. What an incredible thing to witness as each week a different person or family cooked us food, gave us a gift card, or brought us groceries!

For new and deepening friendships, like you uniting me and Hope so that, as new widows, we could work through our grief together. For having Melanie share advice and support as a more experienced widow. For Richard who kept me laughing and encouraged during my weekly hair appointments. And for Donna, whose support was much needed, highly appreciated, and an incredible blessing!

For male role models like my dad, my friend Chris, Ralph's friend Doc, and my brother-in-law Antwione who kept connecting with my boys, showing them that actions speak louder than words.

For fraternities and sororities showing how much good these organizations can do. Besides showing up at the funeral in full force, my sorority sisters brought meals and fellowship, while Ralph's fraternity brothers showed my sons the power of their brotherhood by acknowledging their friend, Ralph, on his birthday, sharing great stories, and providing college funds in remembrance and support. How powerful!

For all the friends that it would take books to name and thank—whether sharing ideas on how we could recover financially, sending an unexpected note, or just showing love via their words and actions!

**For Faith**:

For the people like Lisa and Joy who you put in my life to be spiritual guides and my pastor, John K. Jenkins Sr., of First Baptist Church of Glenarden, whose teachings and straight talk have allowed me to learn so much about you and who I am in you.

For my '4 Ladies of God' prayer group (Lisa, Monika, and Delores), which continues to uplift me (and each other) while glorifying your name.

And most of all, for You, dear Lord, for being the small voice inside that I sometimes couldn't hear but often could feel. Your presence in me and in my life has sustained me in the valley and left me with eternal promises of better days to come. Thank you for all you are and for all you mean to me and the world. Thank you also for loving me in spite of myself!

Dear Lord, I know I have so much more to learn. I know the trials I have faced will not be my last. I know you have something special planned for my life and for the lives of every single one of your children. Please continue to help us all to make it through. Help us turn to you. Please continue to put people in our lives who will help us through our pain so that we will, in turn, reach out to others and help them through their pain. At the same time, thank you for all the special people you already placed into our lives, no matter how long or short our time with them. Thank you for the family and friends who really get it and who've reached out to do something to make the lives of the hurting better. Whether it's a word of encouragement or an act of kindness and selflessness, these are people who show your love for us. Thank you for listening to me and loving me despite all my craziness and confusion. Thanks for seeing me through! Finally, thank you for giving me hope! Despite all the pain, my hope for today and tomorrow remains strong. I look forward to continually getting to know and love you more deeply in the days, months, and years to come!

**My Reflections**:

I find incredible peace and hope reading the journal entry above. Historian and author Alice Morse Earle once wrote, "The clock is running. Make the most of today. Time waits for no man. Yesterday is history. Tomorrow is a mystery. Today is a gift. That's why it is called the present." What an appropriate thought for both Survivors and Supporters. Those who have died are part of our history and that history will never be erased. No one can take away our good memories and the contributions made by someone who has died. At some point, it will be necessary to turn away from constantly looking back and instead carry our loved ones in our hearts as we appreciate today and have hope for tomorrow. Whether or not we're grieving, we sometimes have a tendency to focus solely on yesterday or tomorrow. However, having a true appreciation for today may allow each of us to live fuller and more meaningful lives. That gift can benefit not only you, but also your friends, family, and perhaps, the world.

**Survivor Strategies**:

Think: What have you overcome? What has allowed you to heal? When you look at your life today, what do you feel really good about? How can you make the most of today?

Do: Create a list of things you can do to get the most out of each day, as well as a list of what you'd like to accomplish in the future. Then do it.

**Supporter Strategies**:

Think: How have you helped the Survivor to heal? How are you feeling about your contributions? How are you feeling about your own grief? What do you feel most grateful for today?

Do: Create a list of things you can do to get the most out of each day, as well as a list of what you'd like to accomplish in the future. Encourage the Survivor to do the same. Then encourage each other in achieving those goals.

**Your Reflections**:

What's on your mind and in your heart after reading this entry and pondering the questions? In light of this, what will you do?

# CHAPTER 31

# "AFTER WORDS" FROM A SURVIVOR

MY grief is not done. That's because life isn't nearly as tidy as I'd like it to be, and grief is a process that often takes longer than a few months and/or a collection of journal entries. When I read back over my entries in this book, my heart rises and falls with each emotion expressed, each milestone reached, each retelling of a difficult moment, and each realization that I will make it through this. While my journal entries ended on a very positive note, they reflect my state of mind at particular moments in time and not a fairy tale ending. I still experience both high points and low moments when it comes to my grief. That does not mean I am not healing, nor does it mean I am a basket case. It only means that I am human and a wonderful work in process. It has taken me a lifetime to accept and embrace that fact!

As you read my entries, there may have been times when you may have wanted to shake me, hug me, yell at me, pray for me, or take a variety of other actions in response to my words. Those are very natural responses. Please know that I am continuing to take the steps necessary to heal. Whether that's continuing to write, therapy, support groups, friends, or something else, I am committed to managing my grief in a way that's healthy for both me and my family. And now, I want to share with you, the reader, some additional words of wisdom garnered after my many encounters with grief and after reflecting on all of my journal entries. I thought it may be helpful for me to address a few of the questions people have asked me. In sharing, I am not trying to speak for all grieving people, but instead am speaking for just one grieving widow, mother, niece, and daughter.

Now that it's been over a year since Ralph died, how are you doing?

*The answer to that question depends on what mask I'm wearing when the question is posed. When I have my "Sarah Superwoman" mask on, I tell people that I'm doing better than I could be doing (always looking for the up side). When I have my "Sally Sensitive" mask on, I just say I'm doing great, because I'm not sure the person really wants to know the answer to that question. And when I'm wearing my "Sydney Sincere" mask, I say I'm making it from moment to moment, balancing the lows that come with missing someone I can never get back and the highs that come from continuing to live and maneuvering through new territory. People think masks are negative; however, I think they can sometimes help to protect us (as long as they're not overused). I try not to use those masks as barriers to keep me from connecting with sincere people. So, I'll tell you that I'm still missing my husband (and my other loved ones) and am okay with that as it's a natural part of my recovering from loss.*

What about this latest grief process has surprised you?

*As much as I've learned about grief and the fact that there's no time limit on our healing process, I automatically assumed that I was past the greatest part of my pain after the one year anniversary of Ralph's death. But I wasn't. That fact slapped me in the face when I participated in a support group meeting as part of a graduate course and the feelings just poured out. It was a pivotal turning point, because I realized how much I was still struggling. In fact, I came to the conclusion that I really needed professional help in this next stage of my journey of adapting to life without my husband and getting through a tremendous amount of fear and anger. Actually, in hindsight I'm also surprised that I didn't seek therapy for me and the boys earlier.*

What's been a challenge for you?

*I have many challenges, but the biggest one involves living in the past and deifying my loved ones who have died. I often find myself thinking about how life would be perfect if only____ (fill in the blank) would be here. I also think about how perfectly that person would have handled different situations that I must face alone. Dealing with life in this way doesn't make things better for me. Instead, it makes my sadness greater. It also takes away the humanness that made my loved ones special. So, I must constantly remind myself to break free of this thinking by celebrating my loved ones for who they really were and celebrating myself for the person I'm growing to be.*

What's the easiest part for you?

*The easiest part is learning new things and reaching out to help others. Because those are two of my favorite activities, it makes sense that I'm passionate about using my experiences with grief to educate and support others!*

What are your coping strategies?

*My coping method is strongly dependent on the situation. As my journal entries indicate, writing has been a huge part of my healing. I've also benefited from time spent with friends and family, laughter, screaming, walking, acting silly, shopping (although I have to temper this), mini-vacations, reading, Bible study, and more. My philosophy is that if it makes you feel better and it's not damaging to your physical, emotional, spiritual, or financial health, then go for it!*

What's the best way for someone to support you today?

*Make yourself available, reach out even when you're uncertain, forgive me on my bad days, let me know when I'm totally out of line, pray for me, and, most of all, do what's on your heart!*

What additional thoughts would you share with other Survivors?

*On this grief journey, I have lost old friends and I have gained new ones. I have lost myself (at least the person I thought I was), and I have adapted and evolved into the person I am today. I've let go of old dreams and grasped on to new ones. This period of mourning has strengthened me, weakened me, jaded me, and fueled my passion. It has included days when I've awoken with indescribable sadness deep within my heart, yet other times when I've gone to sleep feeling peace, encouragement, and love. This grief journey is like no other. It will be what we make it to be and what it is destined to be. I pray that you will understand and embrace that, then reach out to a Supporter or two to help you through this journey. If you have no one to reach out to, reach out to me. If I can do anything for you, please do not hesitate to contact me at denise@2Grieve2Gether.org.*

# CHAPTER 32

# "AFTER WORDS" FROM A SUPPORTER

IN this book, I've spoken numerous times about the support I received as I grieved. While my cousin, Joy, is my blood relative, that title didn't obligate her to play the special role she took on. It was her choice to be a dependable friend who would not let me fall. I've often wondered whether I would have been as sensitive to her needs if the tables had been turned.

When I lost my mother, Joy was just twenty-eight years old and was in the midst of planning a wedding. Yet, she jumped into the role of encourager and supporter. At the same time, she gave me tough love when I needed it by telling me when my behavior was not aligned with who she knew me to be. In other words, she did not allow me to use my grief as an excuse. Many times, that which looks so natural, takes hard work and practice. As I reflect on the many ways she helped me, I commend my cousin for her efforts and encouraged her to share her wisdom with the readers of this book.

In this chapter, I've posed a few questions to her and recorded her insightful answers below:

You were only twenty-eight when I lost my mom, yet you supported me. How did you know what to do?

*I didn't. Looking back, I guess I did whatever felt natural to do. Your mom died three weeks before my wedding, so it was chaotic trying to reach out to you and still coordinate dress fittings, rehearsal dinner, etcetera. I remember trying to reach out in a hopelessly awkward way, feeling guilty because I was happy about my wedding and still had my mom, and yet you were grieving and still supportive of me. You even continued as my matron of honor. If I did do anything right it could have been because of our friendship and my love for my aunt.*

How did your approach change over the years as you helped me through multiple losses?

*It wasn't conscious. Each loss was tragic and sudden and different, so I imagine each reaction was also. I can say I felt a degree of your pain each time, because I could see how much you were suffering. I just wanted to do something to help you.*

What have you learned about grief over the years?

*That it is a process, and there aren't a magical number of months or years to feel better. There is just time and more time. The intensity of the grief might ease, but the process will be lived out until the day we die. Grief comes in all forms to all people, so there's not one way to respond to it. There was a degree of fear once I realized that, because it tells me that there is nothing I can do but continue the process of trying to help and then trust that process.*

What have you learned about yourself?

*I've learned that sometimes when I feel that my actions are worthless, they really have helped. I've also learned that I should always follow my gut instinct and not assume that the person grieving will not receive my efforts with gratitude.*

As one of my key supporters, you poured so much into me. How did you "refill your own cup" so that you still had time and energy to give to the other parts of your life (like your children, job, church, other friends, etc.)?

*I replenish myself by doing the things I genuinely love to do. I am inspired when I go to church; there's something about worshiping God in the presence of other believers that speaks to me. I am inspired when I go to Barnes and Noble and curl up in a chair and read. I am inspired when I take the children window shopping and we laugh and dream about things we'd purchase if money were plentiful. I am inspired when I walk into a flower shop. I am inspired when I go to Lowes or Home Depot. I am inspired when I can spontaneously have lunch with good friends who make me laugh. Most recently, I am inspired when I finish my walk in the mornings. All these sorts of things continued to fill my cup, as they always have sustained me, and make it possible for me to reach out to help others.*

As you look at ways you were able to help me over the years, is there anything you wish you would have done differently?

*I wish I would have listened more. I'm not sure if that would have made any difference in your grieving process, but listening is something I yearn to perfect. I am a talker so I have to make a conscious effort to listen. Maybe listening more intently would have caused me to support you in a different and better way.*

What advice would you give to someone who's trying to support a friend, co-worker, or family member through a loss?

*Be present and show up, even if you don't know what to say. If you live too far away, call. In addition, watching and listening closely will open other doors for you to help serve others.*

Knowing that I'm still on my grief journey, is there any additional advice you would give me?

*As a dear friend tells me, be gentle with yourself. Also, recognize that grief is a journey and a process.*

Finally, is there anything else that's on your mind?

*Nope! (smiles)*

# CHAPTER 33

# GENERAL THOUGHTS ON GRIEVING

NO list could ever be complete when it comes to grieving, nor will every item on a list apply to everyone. However, it's helpful to start somewhere. Hence, the lists below include a message to both Survivors and Supporters. These lists were born out of my experience when my son died. Since then, others have shared their ideas with me and some have been included below. These are general thoughts to keep in mind when helping yourself and/or others. Hopefully, they'll get you thinking and spark other ideas as you make your way through the grief process.

## FOR SURVIVORS:

1. **Be gentle with yourself.** Don't expect too much too soon. That includes having the perfect reaction or a fixed healing time. Just commit to working through things moment by moment.

2. **Open yourself up to others** (i.e. don't cut yourself off). Relationships are key and grieving is impossible to do alone.

3. **Let people know if they've touched you in some way.** Many times, when a loved one dies, we regret the things we were never

able to share with him or her. While we can't go back in time, we can take time out for the friends and loved ones who are still alive. Thank them now while you have a chance.

4. **Don't be afraid to ask for what you need.** Often, we don't want to bother others. However, they're often willing yet unsure about how to help us, which often makes our requests a gift to them.

5. **Show appreciation for the support and gifts you receive.** People don't always know whether their gestures had the desired impact. Whether it's a call or a note (when you have the energy to do so), let them know what their actions meant to you.

6. **Document your journey via journals, voice recordings, etcetera.** The process of recording your thoughts often becomes a key part of your healing, because it allows you time for expression and reflection.

7. **Find helpful resources** (Internet, books, counselors, support groups, etc.). Our Web site (www.2Grieve2Gether.org) will help you get started in this area.

8. **Work on projects that honor your loved one's memory.** This allows you to put positive energy into something meaningful and lasting.

9. **Protect your time and feelings as appropriate.** Don't feel that you have to make time for everyone or have to subject yourself to people and situations that will make you feel worse.

10. **Allow yourself to experience a range of emotions.** When you have moments of happiness, sadness, anxiety, stress, laughter, and so forth, know that it's okay to feel and just let it out. In

doing so, you avoid the build-up and eventual explosion that comes from holding in everything.

11. **Find constructive ways to express your feelings.** Whether it's writing, talking to a friend, artwork, or another form of expression, look for ways to share what's in your heart and mind.

12. **Forgive people's insensitivity.** No one, including you, is perfect in their response to others. So, if others forget to be sensitive to your loss, go easy on them while appreciating those who actually remember.

13. **Forgive people's absence.** Upon hearing of a loss and/or attending a funeral, people make a lot of promises about being there for you. Unfortunately, life goes on, and they often forget what they said. Know that if you have one or two people, along with your faith and other resources, to lift you up, that's more than enough.

14. **Forgive yourself.** It's easy to blame yourself for all the things you should have done or said to your loved one who has died. No one is perfect. As such, forgive yourself and work to let go of regrets.

15. **Pray continually for yourself and others.** Survivors, Supporters, and everyone in between can benefit from this selfless gesture!

# FOR SUPPORTERS:

1. **When in doubt about what to say, just be there or tell them you care.** A grieving person needs more than your silence. He needs your connection.

2. **Replace clichés with thoughtful words from your heart.** Express yourself in calls, visits, hand-written notes, cards, and other meaningful gestures.

3. **Don't avoid the person because you don't know what to say.** Share any feelings of uncertainty and ask for patience as you try to help.

4. **Ask the person how she's doing and mean it.** Be willing to listen and provide support.

5. **Understand that there are many ways to reach out** (meals, flowers, donations, visits, memorial gifts, etc.). Think about what may be helpful and then do it.

6. **Take initiative.** Instead of making the Survivor contact you (i.e. "call me if you need anything"), go to that person, suggest ideas, or just act on what you feel is right.

7. **Don't end your support right after the funeral.** There will be many holidays and tough times when Survivors will need support. Invite them places, call or do other things to let them know you remember and care.

8. **Be sensitive to the Survivor's needs.** He may not be himself during this period. Exercise patience, love and understanding as much as possible.

9.  **Don't take things the Survivor says or does personally.** Know that she is hurting and may lash out at those closest to her. Your empathy, tolerance, and mercy will help her heal.

10. **Don't overextend yourself so much that you burn yourself out and can't effectively help the Survivor.** Only take on what you can manage, especially if you are also grieving.

11. **If you're supporting a Survivor in a big way, make sure you have support also.** Surround yourself with a few people (friends or professionals) who can be sounding boards, confidantes, and stress relievers.

12. **Don't create extra work for the Survivor.** Survivors have so much on their minds and so many tasks to accomplish. Don't add to that by asking them to call you back or do other work.

13. **If a Survivor reaches out to you, reach back.** It may have taken a lot of effort for him to ask for help, so, whenever possible, find realistic ways to accommodate and/or support him.

14. **Know that the role you play in helping a Survivor is a very special part of the healing process.** It's not about being a perfect friend or following some script. Instead, it's about genuinely being a friend who tries and succeeds in helping.

15. **Pray for the Survivor and for yourself.** It will give you strength, direction, and peace.

# CHAPTER 34

# IDEAS ON HELPING SURVIVORS

**S**UPPORTERS want to help a person who's experiencing the pain of grief. The problem is that they're not mind-readers, and they may be unsure about what to do. How much is too much? What is too little? When is the right time to reach out? When you do, what's most comforting? These are just some of the questions that a potential Supporter may have. Sometimes, in the face of uncertainty, they are paralyzed and do nothing. Other times, they ask the Survivor to tell them what to do. While some Survivors will have the presence of mind to do so, others can't think straight and won't be able to tell Supporters what they need. Included below are five themes related to reaching out. The first five suggestions under each category are for Supporters and the last tip is for Survivors.

- **Regular Contact**: Keep in contact on a regular basis, especially after most people have forgotten about the Survivor. Sample suggestions include:

  - Send cards every few months.
  - Forward inspirational messages to let him know you're thinking of him.
  - Call for no specific reason (just because).
  - Call her back if she doesn't return your call.

- Ask if you can just visit and spend some time together.

**Survivors**: Don't be afraid to reach out to others. People can help you through the healing process!

- **Tributes & Remembrances**: Find a memento for the Survivor or another way to acknowledge the loved one. Sample suggestions include:

  - Write a poem or song.
  - Select jewelry in memory of the loved one (may even consider having it engraved).
  - Find a picture frame to hold the loved one's photo.
  - Make a donation to charity in memory of the loved one.
  - Help the Survivor make a memory book.

**Survivors**: These are also things you can do on your own and/or initiate with your family and friends.

- **Acts of Service**: Do something to give the Survivor one less thing to worry about or to take their mind off their pain. Sample suggestions include:

  - Cook or purchase a meal and take it to the person/family.
  - Give them a gift certificate for a meal (or invite them to dinner).
  - Help them to clean their home (or offer a gift certificate).
  - Offer to run errands for them.
  - Ask them to join you on a day trip.

**Survivors**: Reaching out to serve others sometimes takes your mind off your own pain. Volunteer.

- **Resources**: Help Survivors find resources to deal with what they're going through. Sample suggestions include:

  - Purchase or recommend a helpful book or journal.
  - Let the Survivor know about relevant support groups.
  - Put the Survivor in contact with people you know who've had similar losses.
  - Share your own stories and/or experiences.
  - Ask your pastor or other clergy to visit the family.

  **Survivors**: As you learn and grow, you can give a wonderful gift by becoming a resource for others.

- **Creativity**: Try to think of anything that would be helpful to you in that situation. Sample suggestions include:

  - Provide something that will help them to just get away (i.e. tickets to an event, etc.).
  - Orchestrate ongoing visits, meals or other acts of kindness by family and friends (a caravan of caring).
  - Check in with the Survivor and ask her to share one realistic thing that would make her smile.
  - Find resources to develop your knowledge (you may find ideas and advice in books).
  - Work with other Supporters to coordinate assistance and ensure that a variety of the Survivor's needs are met.

  **Survivors**: Find creative ways to help yourself and to reach out to others.

CHAPTER 35

# More Resources and Ideas

T HESE ideas will provide more specific ways for Supporters to reach out to Survivors (and even for Survivors to thank Supporters). Please visit our Web site at www.2Grieve2Gether.org to get more detailed information.

1.  **Websites** – Investigate Internet resources that may provide helpful information. You can find an initial list of sites at www.2Grieve2Gether.org.

2.  **Books** – In addition to providing valuable information, books can also be used as a means of escape, saying thanks, and much, much more. Visit www.2Grieve2Gether.org to get started.

3.  **Music** – Music has a way of touching someone's heart and lightening their burden. Buy or put together a CD as a way to reach out. A list of uplifting songs can be found at www.2Grieve2Gether.org.

4.  **Scriptures or Affirmations** – Based on the person's belief system, either a scripture or affirmation can serve as a way to provide hope, comfort, and/or encouragement. A list of relevant scriptures can be located at www.2Grieve2Gether.org.

5.  **Visits** – Sometimes time is the greatest gift you can give.

Whether you're watching television together, rocking on the porch, or just sitting in silence, the time you may spend together could be priceless.

6. **Personalized Gifts** – Whether you include the loved one's name or that of the Survivor or Supporter, a personalized gift is a great way to add an extra special touch.

7. **Scrapbook** – Start a memory book with photos and encouraging words.

8. **Handwritten Notes** – Be original in sharing your thoughts and words of encouragement.

9. **Babysit** – Offer to take the kids (or pets) off of their hands for a little while.

10. **Foods/Meals** – Make it so the family doesn't have to worry about breakfast, lunch, or dinner, especially in those early days when they have so much to do and work through.

11. **Restaurant** – Pick them up and take them out to dinner or provide a gift card for the future.

12. **Memory Box** – Create a special box to store cards, pictures and special tributes.

13. **Group Activities** – Gather together people who care about the Survivor and arrange a game night or some other group activity.

14. **Telephone Calls** – Offer to make calls to the funeral home, benefits administrator, and so forth.

15. **Records Management** – Help the Survivor to put her financial and personal information in order.

16. **Scholarships or Community Funds** – Start or contribute to a fund in a loved one's name.

17. **Jewelry** – Get a piece of jewelry that symbolizes the Survivor's loved one.

18. **Plants** – Ask to plant a flower or tree at the person's home in honor of the loved one.

19. **Charity** – Contribute money to a charity in the loved one's name.

20. **Recognize Holidays** – Do something to mark Christmas, Valentine's Day, Mother's Day, Father's Day, and so forth.

21. **Mark Anniversaries** – Remember the Survivor on the loved one's birthday, anniversary, and date of death.

22. **Tributes** – Find figurines, religious items, or other tokens/items of remembrance.

23. **Balloon Release** – Purchase balloons commemorating each year in the person's life and release them into the sky (you can even add special notes or pictures to them).

24. **Poem/Song** – Write a poem or song for the Survivor and then print it and put it in a frame.

25. **Activities** – Invite the Survivor along to a play, picnic, or another activity that will get her out of the house.

**26. Home Upkeep** – Cut his grass, clean his home, or pay someone to do that so the Survivor doesn't have to worry about it.

**27. Lodging** – Offer a place for the Survivor to stay that allows him to have a refuge and have someone take care of him for a short time.

**28. Check-in Calls to the Kids** – Get the kids' cell phone numbers and just call or text them to see how they're doing or to see how their day is going.

**29. Year of Outreach** – Simply send the Survivor a card (or make some other gesture) once per month to acknowledge the fact that she is still in your heart and mind.

**30. Regular Walks or Other Activities Together** – The cost is free, but the benefit is priceless if you can get the Survivor out of the house and exercising as a way to fellowship and get healthy at the same time.

# CHAPTER 36

# THOUGHTS ON WHAT YOU MAY NOT WANT TO SAY OR DO

FOR **SURVIVORS:** When you're hurting, the people who truly care about you want to help. However, they often don't know what to do to assist you. As such, they'll sometimes need your guidance. That includes being willing to ask for what you need. At times, we don't want to tell people what we need out of embarrassment or a desire to keep people away. During the grief process, there's no need for that. So, whenever possible, eliminate some of the following excuses and rebuffs from your vocabulary:

1. **I didn't want to bother you.** Sometimes the greatest gift you can give to others is to allow them to help you. It's not a bother; it's an honor.

2. **I figured you'd be busy.** Everyone is busy, but they can always make time for important people and things. Allow them to help.

3. **I can do it myself.** That may be true, but it's not the point. You may not have your usual level of energy or focus, so try to allow others to help.

4. **I'll just get to it later on my own.** Putting things off is a formula for forgetting or for gaining a mountain of work. Avoid procrastination and accumulation by just saying yes.

5. **I didn't think you'd be willing to help me with that.** Well, now you know that they are willing to help. So, take them up on it!

6. **I didn't know you really meant it when you offered to help.** Some may not be sincere, but many are. Say yes to help; they'll let you know if things have changed.

Equally important is what you say to yourself. It can be easy to fill our minds with negative and false messages. As such, be careful what you think about and try to avoid thoughts such as these:

7. **No one really cares about me.** There has to be someone who cares. While people may show their caring in different ways, it exists so be on the lookout.

8. **I don't have any true friends.** Similar to the statement above, remember not to dismiss people too quickly.

9. **If you really cared, you would have** ... (fill in the blank). Remember that people show they care in a variety of ways. In addition, there are different levels of friendship.

10. **My loved one died because I am being punished**. Avoid taking on such a huge and erroneous burden. Rather, think about the other side of the coin: all the great reasons why you were blessed to have your loved one in your life.

11. **No one understands**. Someone does. Your challenge is to find

that person. This may occur via support groups, friendships, or other resources.

12. **I can't make it through this.** You are stronger than you think you are (as trite as that sounds). Take one day (and sometimes one moment) at a time. In addition, reach out for help.

13. **I'm never going to feel better.** Never say never. Over time, you will develop skills and identify resources that can help you navigate through the grief process and your life's journey.

14. **I'm the only one going through something like this.** Rarely is one alone in their experiences. The Internet and related Web sites make it even easier to find people with common experiences and struggles. Search for them.

15. **I don't need anyone else.** Sharing your experiences, burdens, and triumphs as you grieve is an effective part of the healing process. Grieving together is what this resource is all about.

**FOR SUPPORTERS:** "Call me if you need anything" can be one of the least helpful phrases to say to someone who's hurting. Why? Because it has become a cliché and it puts the responsibility of reaching out on the person who's hurting. Although it has good intentions, it can be frustrating and discomforting to a person who hears it over and over again. Because clichés are often at the top of our minds, the following are some replacement phrases and alternate thoughts to help you refrain from making a bad situation worse:

**Things Supporters may say and phrases that might work better:**

1. **"Call me (or let me know) if you need anything."**
   Alternative: "What do you need?" (If they say nothing, you could say: "Here's something I'd like to do.")

2.  **"I know she's got a lot of folks around her now. I'll just call her later."**
    Alternative: "I know she's got a lot of folks around her now, but I'll still stop by and give her a quick hug."

3.  **So what really happened?**
    Alternative: This is an intrusive question. If the survivor wants to share details with you, she will. Otherwise, don't ask.

4.  **"God wouldn't give you more than you can bear." Or "God knows best." Or "Your loved one's in a better place."**
    Alternative: These phrases can sound trite when you're not the one hurting. Just let the Survivor come to a conclusion like this on his own.

5.  **"You'll need to be strong for the kids/your mom/your family, and so on."**
    Alternative: No one needs expectations placed on them in the midst of grieving. Instead, you could tell the person that you'd like to be strong for them.

6.  **"This is so shocking. I never would have expected this."**
    Alternative: The Survivor is probably more shocked than you are and is unlikely to be comforted by this statement. Just tell them you're sorry for their loss and its suddenness (if that applies).

7.  **"What are you going to do now?"**
    Alternative: Grief clouds the mind, and a Survivor is often not in a position to answer this question, especially in the early days.

8.  **"It's going to be okay."**
    Alternative: This statement may be true, but, saying it doesn't

make it so. Perhaps you can share what you've learned from your own grief journey or from what you've learned from others.

9. **"Did you get my call? Why didn't you call me back?"**
Alternative: For Survivors, little things can take lots of energy. Don't be offended or remind them if they don't call back. Instead, reach out, call again, and say something like, "I'm just calling to tell you I'm thinking of you."

10. **"I assumed …"**
Alternative: As with any part of life, assumptions are usually not a good idea.

11. **"I didn't call because I didn't know what to say."**

12. **"I didn't call because I knew you had a lot of support."**

13. **"I didn't call because I didn't want to bother you."**

14. **"I didn't call because I figured you'd reach out when you were ready."**

15. **"I didn't call because I was uncomfortable with the fact that I had waited too long to reach out."**
Alternatives to 11, 12, 13, 14, and 15: These can all be excuses for lack of action. As a Supporter, you don't need to have a perfect response. In addition, you shouldn't assume that other people supporting the Survivor are an adequate substitute for your relationship with her. Instead, know that each Supporter is unique in his or her role, and each absence may be felt by the Survivor. Often the Survivor needs and appreciates your presence in whatever form that takes. It may not be enough to just think about them; reach out and make your presence known.

More than that, do so in a way that doesn't make the Survivor have to work for your friendship and/or assistance.

# CHAPTER 37

# CLOSING THOUGHTS

A S I close this resource, I'd like to leave you with a concept that I developed a few years ago. One beautiful morning, I went on a walk around the neighborhood before work. With me was my second son, William, and we talked about how much we were enjoying our time together. It was only a thirty-minute walk, but the amount of energy it gave me and the enjoyment I got from being with William was unbelievable. It was then that I wondered aloud about the merits of making sure I spent at least thirty focused minutes each day building relationships like William and I were doing on that spring morning. Next, I considered the merits of having thirty focused minutes alone each day. That time could simply include thinking, walking, praying, reading, exercising, or any other task that would give me energy, peace, and so forth. During that special walk, the 30Me/30We™ concept was born. I pledged to dedicate thirty minutes each day to self-reflection and self-development, along with another thirty minutes to building closer relationships with my children, husband, extended family, friends, and others who were important to me.

Fast forward several years. While the concept was great, I quickly lost sight of it soon after it entered my mind. However, once the fog of my latest grief journey lifted, it was 30Me/30We™ that gave me part of myself back. For example, today as I ran on my treadmill and imagined the benefits of my exercise, I realized this was the first time in a long time that I granted myself the gift of time. The concept is all about time that enriches my life, replenishes my spirit, reenergizes my body, invigorates my mind, enhances my relationships, and makes me a better person in many ways.

So, my final gift to you is one I'd ask you to give to yourself. Whether you are a Survivor or Supporter, consider the daily practice of time spent on yourself and with those closest to your heart. The amount of time really doesn't matter. What's most important is the focus on being fulfilled and being intentional with your activities. The best part is that it only requires small increments of time! Practicing this concept now with whoever is in your life could reap dividends in the future, especially when you're experiencing a loss or helping someone who's hurting.

May you continue to progress and heal as you make it through the journey called "life." In doing so, remember that with every valley we face and every season of grief we experience, there will also be wonderful peaks, beautiful sunshine, and incredible moments of joy. I have learned that life includes both good and bad times, joyful and painful experiences. How we face those times and how we help each other deal with those experiences makes all the difference! I pray for your continued strength and growth (and hope you'll do the same for me). Take care!

Your friend,
Denise Hall Brown

# About the Author

**D**ENISE Hall Brown grew up in a small town in Maryland. She attended the University of Maryland, College Park, and received a Bachelor of Science Degree in Accounting. She then spent over 20 years working in the Financial Services industry in areas such as Accounting, Human Resources, Training, Diversity, Sales, and Sales Management. During that time, she married her college sweetheart and gave birth to four beautiful sons. Life has been good to her! But it's also been tough as she's dealt with the sudden deaths of loved ones.

Denise believes her life mission is to connect with others who are hurting and, in doing so, to work toward healing together. Her website, 2Grieve2Gether.org, aids in her mission of helping Survivors and Supporters. Most recently, Denise attended Hood College, where she received a graduate certificate in Thanatology, the study of death and bereavement.

Today, Denise lives in Maryland with her three teenage sons.

To connect with Denise or obtain information about 2Grieve 2Gether products, seminars and workshops, see below:

2Grieve 2Gether Inc.
PO Box 625, Frederick, MD  21705-0625
Telephone: 888-378-0202
Email: denise@2Grieve2Gether.org
Web:  www.2Grieve2Gether.org